Get Life Organised

A work-from-home household management guide for business owners

Nic Davies

ISBN13: 9798390353578

Contents

Dedication

To Adrian. We are, without a doubt, a true A-Team, having each other's backs and taking turns to lift each other when we fall. Some days, I feel like we're on a seesaw in the harshest of playgrounds. One day, we'll step off, make our way to the top of the climbing frame and enjoy the view together.

Thank you

For having faith in me whilst I build a legacy;

For giving me space to be who I am;

For making sure I know that I am loved;

For taking on absolutely everything at Davies HQ while I've finished writing this book. I promise the next one will be easier.

Love you xx

To Emma and Cameron - all grown and flown. The Mothership is always here for refuelling and recharging, whenever you need it.

To Alfie, Tom, Grace and William, showing the courage of lions in achieving so much and growing into young adults with dignity and resilience.

To Amelia, Isabel, and Lewis – thank you for giving Nana Nic the motivation to rewrite the script.

For my dad whom I miss more than anything, who first planted the seed of being able to do things in a different way. To be able to work for ourselves and create our own reality.

To my virtual village of amazing business peers and mentors. For each and every one of you who has spent time with me on calls and in person. We learn together, we grow together, and we rise together. Without you, none of this would be happening.

Foreword

"Nic, the most organised, the most resilient, the warmest human. Nic gives me inspirational strength in her demeanour each time we connect. Life likes to throw the whole kitchen sink at Nic, Nic catches it, organises it, and then shows the rest of us how to handle business without breaking a sweat."

Dawn Baxter

Founder of Beyond The Dawn Digital

Preface

As a young child, I played with wooden bricks - building them, lining them up and creating patterns with them, all neat and tidy. For my fourth birthday, I got the Kenner Family Treehouse, with the pushdown canopy - my first introduction to running a home.

As I got older, playing cards were my new construction material, seeing how many I could stack before they fell. I quickly learned these had to be perfectly organised otherwise it wouldn't work.

During my first year of high school, I was mocked for bringing all my schoolbooks with me every day. But it was the only way to make sure I didn't forget anything. I hated disorganisation and knew my anxiety wouldn't cope with being in trouble for forgetting. In later years, forgetting my PE kit was a frequent occurrence but that didn't bother me for some reason.

I yearned for the pencil cases the popular girls had - neat compartments, with colour-matching pens to match their perfect handwriting. As a left-hander, I always smeared ink over the page. I pretended not to care.

At eighteen, I worked at a hotel near the Lake District. My job was to help wherever I was needed. I soon realised I could turn my hand to all kinds of work. I covered reception, laundry, housekeeping, cleaning, working behind the bar, as a kitchen porter and assistant chef or waiting on in the dining room. It was here I started creating efficient work systems. The head waitress didn't seem to know what she was doing, despite finishing catering college, and would take over two hours to serve three courses to fifty-five guests. Most of the food was cold, orders were wrong and it was a total disaster. She left and I was put in charge, even though I had no formal training.

Whilst observing the problem, I worked out the solution. We had gone from four waitresses to two, just me and another girl. I told her my new plan and she agreed to give it a go. We served all fifty-five guests three courses within one hour. No one was rushed, all orders were correct and the food was hot. I'd halved the time it took with half as many staff.

As a single parent at nineteen, being organised was essential. I was no longer just looking after myself, but a tiny human too. Parenthood is a shock to the system at any age and to the most secure of relationships. I was raising my daughter with no clue what I was doing. I got things right; I got things wrong. It was a major rollercoaster of learning.

After being burgled by my neighbours, I swapped houses with another council tenant via the mutual exchange scheme. I moved across town to an estate I'd never heard of, registered my daughter at a nursery in town and began college, learning how to type and use computers. I had to get to the nursery in town, then back out of town to college and then do it all again in the afternoon. Sometimes I'd walk home from town, doing the shopping on the way, making the most of the cheaper shops in the town centre. I created routines to keep myself occupied and fit. I kept myself busy until I got back to employment.

A few years later, married and with my second child, I volunteered with the local community group alongside parenting. I learned so much and I enjoyed my role in helping set up a new community centre. My confidence soared. I knew that I was here to make a difference in the world and not just be a casual bystander.

Many house moves later, divorced and raising teens, I met Adrian, a dad of eight, who was juggling time with his kids at the weekends and the odd weeknight in between. After six months of friendship, something clicked and six months after that, he moved in.

We had no idea what lay ahead. After another six months, we became full-time parents together for his younger children after their mum died. All the previous times in my life when I'd thought I was busy were a drop in the ocean compared to the tsunami that hit us. Living in firefighting mode for months on end, we navigated one hell of a storm. Appropriate family support was non-existent, we were on our own. We got some stuff right and a lot of stuff wrong, but kept going regardless, and are now rebuilding our lives after losing everything – our home, health, sanity, and almost our lives. I reached my lowest point in 2020, with a heart attack at the age of 45. I'm just so grateful I'm here now and don't intend on making the same mistakes that led me to burnout.

My inspiration for this book is down to how many people said to me things like:

"I don't know how you do it"

"How do you manage to do it all"

"I could never do that. I wouldn't know where to start"

"It's a good job you've got broad shoulders"

...except my shoulders are no broader than anyone else's. There's always a price to pay for pushing to (and beyond) the limits. Whilst I don't have all the answers, this book is a good start to spinning the multiple plates of life without completely losing yourself in the process, knowing which ones to treat like fine bone china, and which ones you can let fall.

Nic x

Introduction

You've found yourself squashed and burdened under the weight of responsibilities in life.

Life looks different from how you imagined. You may be in a relationship, or single. You may have kids, or not. Maybe grandchildren, stepchildren, a big, blended family? You might be caring for your parents who now require extra support from you.

You might be in employment or employment with a side hustle. Maybe you're juggling studying alongside work and family commitments or you're a full-time business owner, working your way to the Holy Grail of financial freedom and flexibility.

Whatever's going on in life, you're struggling with the day-to-day, and need help in finding that light at the end of the tunnel. No matter how hard you try, you're making little progress toward that easier life you promised yourself.

Everyone wants something from you, you're giving and giving, and your cup is almost empty, but you still get up every day and keep going.

As a kid, you couldn't wait to grow up, and as a bored teenager, the only thing keeping you going was a yearning for all the freedom that adults appeared to have, but now you are an adult, you don't know what true boredom feels like anymore because there is always something to do, and most of it isn't very exciting. Every part of your day is full of home and family responsibilities, intertwined with running a business.

There's a little voice whispering to your overloaded conscience, making sure you don't forget that whilst it's all well and good you've taken time out to read this book, you need to remember lots of other things too:

- You haven't taken tonight's meal out of the freezer to defrost,

- Your scheduled social media post for today didn't go out and you need to publish it manually,
- You're out of bread again so need to pop to the shops after tea so the kids can have packed lunches tomorrow,
- You didn't cancel that free trial software subscription. The first payment's gone out without you even trying it,
- You wonder if there's enough milk left for breakfast in the morning (if you're lucky, you'll have asked yourself this question before going to the shop for bread),
- You didn't respond to a message yesterday which could potentially result in your next client,
- You forgot to return those clothes you ordered that don't fit properly. You've left it too late for a refund, so that's more clutter, and guilt at wasting cash,
- You're wondering when you'll find time to get a full day to batch-create your newsletters instead of posting on the fly,
- Is it the school parents' evening tonight or tomorrow?

Your brain is at capacity. And it's been there for a long time now, on just the day-to-day stuff that magically comes naturally to all adults (somehow). You've barely started tackling the business project you planned last quarter. Times are testing and you're feeling it.

Your inner monologue nag never ends. It makes sure you remember tasks – but it's usually around 2 am when you've woken up to pee because your bladder works overtime these days. Then you struggle to get back to sleep as your brain has decided now is a good time to think about the to-do list that's floating around in your head because you hadn't written it down. You were sure you'd remember it all.

After a couple of hours of tossing and turning, you get back to sleep, only to wake feeling drained and only getting out of bed on your third and final alarm.

You're in perpetual guilt mode and it feels heavy:

Guilt from throwing fish fingers and chips at the kids again because it's easier than dealing with arguments or cooking from scratch.

Guilt from not ironing the school uniforms again because Sunday evenings have become a painful transition to the busy week ahead.

Guilt from not spending enough quality time with your partner, from not taking care of yourself, knowing what you should be doing and just not having any capacity, time, motivation or energy to do it.

You've stepped into the role of a business owner (whether planned or fallen into via various plot twists) and you're committed to making it work, yet you can't switch off from housework tasks that are within view in every direction at home. When you try to focus on work, the pile of washing catches your eye, so you get up and put it away. After which, you get caught up doing more tasks that you spot need doing.

You suddenly realise you'd started over an hour ago. It's taken longer than the ten minutes you'd anticipated and that's another hour lost on the business today...

Which means you didn't write that sales page or your social media posts. You feel even more guilty! Another day of not being visible in your business and of not getting your offers out. Another day with no money in and you've still not implemented what your business coach has repeatedly suggested you should be doing. You're exhausted and feel like a failure.

Supermarket shelf stacking is starting to feel like a viable option. Why wouldn't it? Consistent income, less stress, and someone else making all the decisions for you. It's very tempting.

Where does this cycle end? Working from home takes a huge amount of discipline and resolve to stay on track and do it consistently. Even the most hardened Entrepreneurs can find themselves preoccupied with cleaning out under the stairs, looking for that one mislaid item.

You clean to avoid tackling the tech problem that will move your business forward. You also become an expert at creating a hundred social media graphics, so you don't have to clean the bathroom.

When you are finally working in flow, you forget to eat lunch and drink water, then teatime arrives and there's nothing prepped. Convenience meals or takeaways become a regular choice.

All this stress and overwhelm is leading one way and it's not going to end well. Not having boundaries, not eating properly, not staying hydrated, not taking breaks, not having a plan, and living in perpetual firefighting mode in all aspects of life... It's the road to burnout.

I know this because I've done it myself.

I've been through extremely testing times over the last few years, none of which I was prepared for - going from running a household of three to a household of eight overnight, having to adapt to this permanent change quickly and with very little warning, learning to care for and raise children of differing ages and needs, adapting to large, blended family life... I've gone through my own burnout journey not once, but three times in total (believe me, you get the message the third time).

I've worked through extreme financial hardship - nano-managing the shopping budget, making meals stretch to feed everyone, sourcing school uniforms with little notice and no money, whilst trying to keep two businesses running, looking after myself, supporting my partner to support his grieving children, and making sure life didn't completely fall apart.

I've made mistakes that have cost me my home and my health. I've been through one of the biggest learning experiences of my life. I'm so grateful that where I'm at today is much more comfortable.

And now, I'm here to help you.

There is no official qualification for managing life and its curveballs, but I do have a wide range of skills, knowledge, and experience. From those, I can help you in your quest to live a more organised and streamlined life.

I say this confidently because I've worked out how to balance a crazy busy life whilst focusing on work projects to fulfil my life goals, and not just make a living serving someone else's dream.

I've learned from all the mistakes so you don't have to. I've learnt to bring together systems and strategies to keep my head above water, thrive, and grow, all whilst knowing the essentials in life are sorted. And they're right here in this book.

Once you've read this book, you'll have a useful toolbox of knowledge and skills to use and refer to, for streamlining your day-to-day life and being able to breathe easier knowing you've got everything in hand.

Imagine how different your days could look:

Having meals planned for the year and knowing you'll rarely run out of ingredients because you're on top of the grocery lists and the cupboards are well stocked.

Doing everything with more ease and flow. Cupboards are no longer overflowing; you find everything quickly and easily. There's no ironing pile seeking your attention, or piles of clutter. You know where everything is. You can find your keys in the morning. Your paperwork is all filed.

There's no last-minute faffing with "dress as a unicorn day" for school. Plans are in place for inset days and you have contingencies for when the kids are off ill. Life feels lighter. Decisions are easier. You have more free time and headspace back for new creative business ideas. Life will never be perfect, but it does feel a lot easier now it's better organised and under control.

I'm a problem solver. A good one. I've worked hard to regain control of my own life through learning and implementing. I've always been able to work things out and find solutions, by observing and then trying things out to see what works. Analysing and streamlining are useful skills for business *and* home.

Perfectionism is unattainable. If that's what you're looking for, this isn't the book for you. As a recovering perfectionist, I can say with confidence that it causes procrastination and overwhelm and nothing gets done.

I've helped clients in streamlining not just their physical environment at home, but also how they approach their day - from what order tasks are done to how they keep momentum when life gets difficult. I help them to realise that while some days are great other days we need someone to hold our hand and let us know it's okay to stop and rest and just pick the baton up again tomorrow.

The biggest breakthrough I help with is knowing that the most important boundaries we can put into place in life are the ones with ourselves. We think of ourselves as superhuman and expect too much of ourselves - that we must always give more than anyone else ever does.

Many of us took the leap from employment to escape workplace bullying, stress, and other difficult working conditions, but by having no plans or structure to work with, we become the worst boss ever to ourselves!

It's time to become your own best friend. Some days that means ignoring the chores and resting, other days it means calling yourself out and keeping yourself accountable. It's a fine balance to be undertaken with love and compassion for ourselves and it's another skill where the work is never *done*.

This book will show you how to approach some of the expectations of modern-day living, whilst still finding time and energy to spend on building and running your business. There are tasks included in every chapter should you wish to do them and there's an accompanying PDF download to help with these available via the QR code at the back of the book.

Without it sounding too boring, you need to run your home like a business. You wouldn't run a business without a strategy, so why do we undertake running our homes without one? Consider what's involved in running a home. It's taken for granted that things just get done.

Think of the main goals as streamlining your life and having your housework on autopilot, with nothing that needs major effort. There's no drama or stress. Everything runs smoothly with ease and flow. Problems are minor and life is good.

For that to happen though, preparation comes first. The planning part takes some time but it's necessary - without a plan, there's no direction. You end up in fire-fighting mode every day, without time to stop and think. This isn't a sustainable way to live.

Think of this book as a guide to creating your own map, and the destination is an organised life that serves you far better than the chaos that's currently in control. Even if you lose your way for a while, it helps you to get back on track. Far better to have a plan and meander from it, than to have no plan at all.

As a business owner, it's harder to separate work from home. Everything rolls into one. We live and breathe our businesses. There's no distinct beginning and end.

There's nothing wrong with that, however, if you're working all the time which then puts your health and relationships at risk, we need to talk.

I'm here to help you work out how to run your home and business together and work towards a fulfilling life that's true to your values.

Are you ready to transform your time and how you spend it? Think of the time spent reading this book and working on the tasks as an investment of your time that you will reap the benefits from. Take some time to plan things out, and you'll be rewarded with more quality time back... and a lot less brain clutter.

Grab yourself a brew, make yourself comfy, turn the page and we'll begin.

Your next step towards getting life organised starts here.

Chapter 1

Rotas And Reality Checks

Spending hours looking for a housework rota to suit a large family resulted in lots of brick walls. There are a lot of good ones out there that may be helpful for others, but they didn't work for us. They didn't account for the size of the household, room numbers, layout, lifestyle, and any other needs.

With so many factors involved in designing a rota, a one-size-fits-all is an impossible task.

You might not want to do an hour of housework every day, or clean at weekends. What about physical limitations? Or just struggling to manage at the best of times? How does a standard rota help? It doesn't work.

And there's no "average" family anymore. With divorce rates increasing, family dynamics change from one household to the next - multiple generations under one roof, blended families with extra kids at weekends, or the kids away visiting absent parents. What about age ranges? What hours do you work? Do you work from home? Are you studying? All these factors can't be covered with one standard system dictated by someone else.

The numbers in our household have changed over the years. We are now *down* to six of us. Life is reasonably stable right now, but we've also two businesses to run and two dogs to care for, and are still working through bereavement, chronic illness, PTSD and post-heart attack recovery. We are one big, complicated, blended family and we need something more tailored to keep life organised.

No one else knows how often we clean the kitchen floor or the skirting boards. Who even makes the rules about how often things should be cleaned and tidied?

The best housework rota you can have is the one you create for yourself. *You* know how often you want or need to clean, not how often others tell you to.

I understand that creating your own rota can take time, particularly a detailed one. Use ready-made rotas as a starting point and tweak them according to the needs of your household but don't expect to find one that suits your needs exactly.

One of the most controversial questions I've seen asked in an online forum is "how often do you change your bedding?" This is met with a diverse range of opinions and unfortunately, judgement if the group or page isn't moderated appropriately.

It's no one else's business how often you change your sheets. Whatever you are comfortable, happy, and safe with is the right answer.

This goes for any household chore. You get to choose when and how often, and it will change over time depending on what's happening in your life. I've had periods where I've been on top of the housework, waking naturally at 6 am every day and having the place sparkling and spotless. I didn't use a rota during that time, I just knew how and when to get on with it with no list to motivate or remind me. Life is a lot different to that now!

I've had other periods when just getting out of bed was too much to deal with. The cleaning had to wait, clutter was piled everywhere and the bathroom had become a health hazard. I've been at both ends of the organised home spectrum and know only too well that our mental and physical health and well-being have a strong impact on what we can do.

I talk a lot about not having things set in stone. The sky won't fall if the housework doesn't get done. Do what you can, when you can, that's all we can ask of ourselves. However, if you do want to set some time aside to create a bespoke chore system for you and your household, it's a worthwhile task. There are a lot of benefits to having one in place:

- You can keep track of what's being done and how often,
- You can identify what's being ignored/forgotten about,
- You can identify who is better at what,
- It can promote teamwork at home,
- It can build a sense of accomplishment (if ticking things off works for you),
- It can provide motivation if lists are your thing,
- You can allocate tasks to other household members more easily,
- It takes thinking on the spot out of the equation, giving you back some headspace.

If you're not one for rotas, tasks and lists however, you may just see drawbacks:

- It puts you under pressure,
- You feel like a failure if you don't complete it,
- You haven't got time to create one,
- Lists/rotas don't motivate you,
- You don't like routine.

It's a double-edged sword but if you've always shied away from creating a rota, or feel that they don't work, I would lovingly ask you to see if this is something you could work on. It might spark an idea for you to do things in a different way. I'm sharing what I've found works for me and I hope it's helpful for you.

HOUSEWORK GOALS

A good starting point is to consider what your ideal living space base point looks like. Be realistic. Is a clutter-free, neutral, minimalist look achievable within your space and family dynamics? I'm a Maximalist at heart. I love vibrant colours and clutter in an organised fashion. I love to see items on display. The pen and pencil pots I have on the shelves behind me in my office space have become legendary on Zoom calls! I keep knitting wool balls in a wide shallow box out on the shelf, all different colours.

These are part of my crafting collection and beautiful, so why not have them out on display? I struggle with remembering what I've got if it's not in my line of sight, but I know others prefer things like these behind cupboard doors. Consider what you want your home to look like, what sort of atmosphere is comfortable and how you want to feel once you've closed the door to the outside world.

I see these as housework goals, which can be a combination of objective and subjective ideas and only you can decide what your housework goals are. You may want to evoke a particular feeling and have specific items away out of sight. Maybe it's just wanting a clean, functional home, or perhaps you want everything streamlined with nothing on show. There are lots of variances between these two as well. We all have our own characters and identity. If we share our living space with others, finding the solution to what we desire and what is realistic can be a balancing act just on its own. Housework goals aren't there to intimidate or demotivate. See them as a guide to what you want to achieve.

I've come up with examples that I want for my home. I feel they are both realistic and achievable, resulting in my top ten goals for our happy home. You could use these as a starting point for your list.

I want my home to be:

1. Reasonably clean and tidy, without being perfectly neat or spotless,
2. Practical for me to work from home efficiently, without impeding home life,
3. Comfortable enough for us to live in, without causing extra stress and anxiety, and for us to make the most of the space available,
4. Somewhere that guests can drop in and feel at ease, without worrying about getting dirt on the carpet (within reason of course!), spilling a drink, or breaking something,
5. To be clean and tidy enough for me not to care what state it's in if unexpected visitors arrive,
6. A space where the floors and other surfaces are free from clutter and we are able to put things away easily when finished with them,
7. Organised enough that I can find something when I need it straightaway,
8. A useful space, with kitchen worktops clean and clear other than small appliances and utensils used regularly, with enough room to prepare food and serve the evening meal,
9. A fresh environment that smells pleasant without the overuse of air fresheners or wax burners,

10. A happy, relaxed and content atmosphere for the whole family to open up and feel like they can be themselves.

Write down your goals and pin them up on the fridge or noticeboard. Think about how you can achieve them if you aren't already doing them. Make sure they are realistic and achievable. This is also a good time to point out that those picture-perfect homes you see on Instagram and Pinterest are most likely staged and aren't realistic as a permanent look in a busy household. There's more than likely stuff piled behind the camera that's been moved while the photo is taken or it's an Airbnb rented out for a photo shoot. Don't believe this is the day-to-day expectation.

FIVE STEPS TO CREATING YOUR HOUSEWORK SYSTEM

My five-step plan can help create a housework rota that is tailored to you and your household. By drilling down, you can make it a fully comprehensive system or, if you don't want to deep dive into such a big task, start small and keep it basic. Add more details later as you have more time and capacity.

Perhaps the kids keeping their rooms clean is an impossible task or physical restrictions prevent you from cleaning the bathroom on a regular basis. It's time to be realistic and know that whilst your home is safe and secure, most tasks can wait.

But it doesn't hurt to have a plan in place, even if it's wishful thinking right now. You can work towards it at your own pace.

This is the plan:

- Step 1 – make a list of all the tasks in your home that you know need doing.
- Step 2 – record how long each one takes to complete.
- Step 3 – write down how often you want to do each task, or how often something needs cleaning/sorting.
- Step 4 – decide how long each day and/or week you want to spend doing the housework.
- Step 5 – create your plan, based on all the above steps.

That sounds so simple, doesn't it? Just five steps and you'll have everything under control.

Clearly not! There's a fair bit of work. But I can walk you through the steps with what I've done to get it working well for us. You'll need to block out planning time and make a commitment to do it. You might decide it's too much faffing about right now. Go as deep as you want with this exercise, or just do a basic task list and see how you go.

If you are serious about putting a long-term system into place though, then you'll need to work through things methodically and be patient. Transitioning from chaos to calm is not an overnight solution, regardless of what you see on TV. Whether you want an immediate overhaul of your housework rota, or you want to implement it slowly over a longer period, this works for both and is easy to refer to once it's done.

It's hard work, but worth it for the long-term benefits, particularly if you're reaching capacity with time and energy in your business and you're working out where to find extra time without outsourcing yet. Think of it as having your home streamlined and your housework on autopilot, freeing up more time to work on your business or spend quality time with family and friends.

The five steps in more detail:

Identify your chores – go around the house with a clipboard, pen, and paper. Write the room name, and starting in one corner, go around the room clockwise and write down all the cleaning and housework tasks you identify. This will take some time, but by the end, you'll have a thorough room-by-room task list. Maybe just do one list per day, so it doesn't become too tedious. Or start with just a few tasks from each room, and add others at a later date if that works better for you.

Time taken to complete - record how long each job usually takes to complete. You'll have a combination of five-minute, ten-minute, fifteen-minute, and thirty-minute jobs. If any jobs take longer than half an hour, split them down into sub-tasks. Be realistic with timings and remember your energy levels will fluctuate, so jobs may take longer on different days. You are the best person to gauge this. If you're unsure how long a task will take, always overestimate so you're never trying to cram too much in.

How often - decide how often you want to complete these chores, or how often you feel it needs doing. If you need guidance on how often a task needs doing then, by all means, Google it and get a feel for what would be a good timescale for you but keep ***your*** time and energy at the focus of this rota. Don't worry about it looking perfect or comparing it to anyone else's. It needs to work around you, your needs, your energy, and your household dynamics.

On your terms – decide how much time you want to or are willing to spend on doing these chores every day, week, fortnight, or month. I'm sure no one wants to spend most of the day cleaning, even more so if you're working or running a business. Set daily time limits depending on your comfort levels (both physical and emotional). Decide a suitable timescale, consider other commitments for each day, and jot down what time it's likely to be. My peak times for housework are around 9 am depending on how my sleep pattern has been and what time I start work, and after 4 pm until teatime. Friday mornings are a good time for me to do extra tidying and cleaning, with all other weekdays taken up with working or running errands.

Create your bespoke rota – look at all the previous points and start drawing together your own rota based on the frequency of tasks you've chosen and what time you have available daily. You may need to adjust the frequency of jobs or break larger jobs down even further to find a balance that works well for you. Spread jobs out so you're not doing too many heavy ones at once. Decide if you're going to block out specific times on certain days or whether you'll slot in housework here and there around work tasks. I find a mixture of both works well for me. If I don't have a call, I use the hour following the afternoon school run for housework. I also do it then because I struggle to focus on work when everyone is home, so I may as well use the time effectively. It's a good segue into the evening, with getting teatime underway and winding down from work.

I appreciate that following the steps is time-consuming and may feel over the top. I've put worksheets in the PDF download that's available using the QR code at the back of the book. These will help you go through the steps.

I stop people in their tracks when I tell them I've got my housework set out for the year. You might be under the impression I thrive on housework. This couldn't be further from the truth. I don't enjoy housework! I'd much rather be working, knitting, drawing, making jewellery, walking along the coastline, or just out and about. My zone of genius isn't scrubbing the kitchen floor. So why do I obsess over housework when I don't enjoy it? The answer is simple. Because I want it over and done with. If I want a clean, functioning home, then it needs to be done. My home isn't pristine and spotless. I have cobwebs in corners, and junk piles here and there. I've got stuff to sort through in the garage, and my work desk is often a disaster zone. I'm realistic with how we live and at this moment in our lives, we're striving for function over form. I'm building a business focused on creating a legacy and for me to be able to do that, my focus is not on perfectly curated interiors right now. It's on functionality and making life easier and more manageable whilst we navigate another busy period in our lives. This will change at some point. We'll find ourselves in our forever home that I can curate and style to suit our personalities and lifestyle. But right now, it's about keeping things simple and focusing on the essentials. If you are in a build and/or growth period of your business, your focus may be similar.

FREQUENCY OF TASKS

I base the repetition of tasks on a one, two, four, or eight-week frequency. The next one is twelve weeks, with other tasks every six months and annually. I find these intervals cover most of what's required to keep on top of the housework and fit in well with each other.

At this level, base things around the weeks of the year. You can break it down further into days once you've got a feel for what jobs go in which week. Your weekly tasks go in first, into each week. For fortnightly tasks, split them into two lists for weeks one and two. With four weekly tasks, create four lists and spread the task across the four weeks evenly. Do the same with eight and twelve weekly tasks. Consider how physically demanding the tasks are. Don't cluster them together if you know they're hard work. What you're working towards is an equal distribution of jobs, so you're not dreading specific weeks. Those are the times you are more likely to avoid doing the work.

An example of how I distribute tasks is defrosting the chest freezer. I schedule this every twelve weeks. I tie it in with restocking it to make the whole process more efficient. We have two fridges; one in the kitchen and one in the garage. They're cleaned fortnightly, but only one at a time. So the kitchen fridge goes into week one, and the garage fridge into week two.

I used to work for the Fire Service and observed practices and routines that made sense to the logical part of my brain. Consider what might happen if the fire appliance (engine) turned up to a call and some equipment wasn't working. It could be a disaster, possibly fatal. To make sure everything was maintained properly, they had Standard Tests.

All Standard Tests were recorded in a large file. Every single piece of equipment, whether it was on the appliance or kept on the station was given a code, a description, and a frequency, or interval of how often it needed to be checked or serviced. As part of the daily crew duties, they checked all the equipment that was programmed in for that day.

The file was full of tables for the recording of dates and signatures. Some equipment was tested daily. Some were scheduled weekly, fortnightly, four-weekly, and so on. The files were a comprehensive rota system and an audit record for if anything did go wrong.

I've taken inspiration from this to create my annual housework rota, which runs continuously, year after year. It might change if we get a new piece of furniture or appliance, when our work routines change, or in response to other external factors. It will certainly change again when we move house. Whilst it's not essential, like testing Fire Service equipment, it's a useful system for anyone who struggles with keeping on top of the housework or can't remember when they last cleaned or serviced something. It's a great resource to check where you're up to and look at what's coming up.

Remember, it can be as simple or as comprehensive as you want. Maybe you could add in all those invisible jobs that no one else seems to be aware of - the ones the House Pixies do! And there'll always be something that gets missed. Think about how often you clean the filter out on the extractor hood. Is this a regular task for you? What about the cupboard under the sink? Or the tops of the kitchen cupboards? When was the last time they were tackled? Dare you even look? It's those kinds of jobs I'm thinking about. Get them programmed into your rota so it's not a dirty gunky surprise when you remember in twelve months' time.

FLEXIBILITY

The rota I've created for myself is well structured, comprehensive, super organised and breaks everything down into detail. I've deliberately designed it this way to have a higher frequency of tasks than I expect to manage. I don't beat myself up about sticking to it so, if for whatever reason they don't get done, it's okay, and they just get picked up next time. In real terms, this means rather than scheduling to do something fortnightly, some tasks are scheduled weekly, that way, if you miss a week, it doesn't matter.

This isn't to put me under pressure, it's a guide. A flexible manual or blueprint on how to keep my living environment organised, clean, tidy and running comfortably.

There's no catching up to do. You either do the chores or you don't, but do be realistic about basic tasks that keep our home environments clean, clear, functioning and safe. You'll need to wash up the dishes every day for tomorrow to be as easy as today but if the bed sheets don't get changed this week, it's not the end of the world. The impact is minimal and life continues as normal.

The way I look at housework, and life generally, is that it's better to have a plan and not stick to it than to have no plan at all.

TRAFFIC LIGHT SYSTEM

The traffic light system is used as a way of dividing a rota in an organised structure to allow for days when we just aren't feeling it. It's not my idea but I have seen it recommended a lot. A quick Google search will show examples of how people are using it.

I believe it was designed for people with chronic illness, particularly when energy levels fluctuate and it's impossible to predict how they'll be from one day to the next, or even on an hourly basis. I know this only too well as I can be in fine fettle one day and unable to function the next. If this happens, the main rota goes out of the window.

Each housework chore is given either a green, amber or red colour, like our traffic light system. Green chores are for when you are in tip-top shape, you feel like conquering the world and you're in good flow physically, mentally, and emotionally. Life is good, you can manage everything. They are also the tasks that get sidelined on amber or red days.

Amber tasks are for when you're feeling okay but you're not on top form. You're not running on empty, but you know if you do too much then you might find yourself in a pain flare, or exhaustion. Amber is your warning to proceed with caution. Don't overdo things by taking on a whole garage declutter over a weekend.

Red tasks are for the days when you are in a flare or can only do the bare minimum. The only tasks to be completed on these days are the ones that are crucial to your day-to-day basic functioning to meet your physiological needs. These might look like keeping the sink clear, but not necessarily clean, and making sure there's a section of clean worktop to prep some food. They don't include vacuuming, cleaning baths or showers, decluttering, or any similar tasks which can wait another day. You will be able to identify your own tasks based on what you usually manage to do when you're not well.

The traffic light system is also useful when you know you'll be busier than normal. The difference here is you can also plan in advance. Take, for example, a product launch for your business, or during school holidays when you know more of your time is taken up with the kids, do you really want to be bothered with sticking to a full rota at these times? During busier times, taking more care of yourself is the priority, and part of self-care is also knocking some of the housework on the head when needed.

Preparation is key. If you know these times are coming – and you will if launches are part of your business strategy - then you can prepare in advance. Make it part of your launch preparation to clear the decks at home. It may mean knocking green tasks on the head for a couple of weeks or making sure a few of the amber tasks are still completed so things don't accumulate.

What we don't want to do is overwhelm ourselves by pushing everything back. Think about what makes life easier on a daily basis, and focus on those. Review your housework rota and start to allocate tasks. Ask yourself how essential they are and colour-code accordingly. Would anyone notice if they didn't get done? Identify which tasks aren't urgent, but need to be kept on top of to make sure things aren't more difficult in a few weeks' time.

To round off this chapter, here are the tasks to consider undertaking:

1. Identify your housework goals. List ten if possible.

2. Work through the five steps to creating your personal rota. Tackle this in whichever way is best suited to you.
3. Identify your traffic light chores. What's essential for daily functioning? What could wait?

For worksheets to help with all of these, get the accompanying PDF download via the QR code at the back of the book.

Chapter 2
Managing Your Time

Time is the most precious commodity we will ever have. Once spent, you can't get it back. Every twenty-four hours marks another day gone in our calendar. Every seven days a week. Every fifty-two weeks a year. Before we know it, our time has flown and we wonder what happened to it.

We should treat our time with the respect it's due. We should be more mindful of how it's spent, and aware of when to slow down, when to step up the pace and when to delegate and streamline difficult tasks.

I've spent my time in different ways throughout my life. I've been super productive and super lazy. I've wasted time on projects that were never going to work and called time on others that felt too difficult when I should have persevered. Some day-to-day tasks are monotonous and boring, but I save those for when I'm not firing on all cylinders or when I need to process my thoughts but also need to feel productive.

There are lots of tools and tips to get your time management under control. A quick Google search will suggest different ways of doing things, all of them right *and* wrong. There is no definitive answer. I can't cover every single tip and tool here because it would take an entire book itself, but I can discuss what works for me and how I do things, to inspire you to find what works best for you.

DIARY MANAGEMENT

The look and feel of brand-new planners bring me joy! The crispness of the paper with blank pages laid out before me awaiting new, exciting plans to be written upon them. Unfortunately, I have never found the perfect layout for me, which is why I'm now creating my own range!

What I really need is an old-fashioned 1980s style Filofax with space for everything. My go-to diary for the last decade has been a WHSmith standard A4, 18-month week to view academic diary. I get it every year because there are no surprises, I know exactly what I'm getting. They go up for sale in June and it's great value to get 18 months' worth of planning pages for a tenner. It runs from the 1st of July through to the 31st of December the following year - fantastic for forward planning on paper.

Whilst marketed as a student academic diary, it's perfect for parents who want to get ahead with recording school holidays as early as possible. It's large enough to write in properly and there's an A5 version if you prefer something more portable.

The downside is that I need to customise it for my needs. I use black drawing pens to put in extra columns and rows into the week to view pages. I've designed a layout that works well for me. It is tedious and time-consuming, but I know I've got the right setup that's going to make life easier. I see it as having a dot grid journal system with a head-start on the layout and I don't need to draw everything from scratch.

BULLET JOURNALLING

The official Bullet Journal system (often referred to as BuJo) was designed by Ryder Carroll who shared the idea in 2013. It's a well-organised and functional way of designing your own planner list from scratch. The original Bullet Journal process focuses on function over form and uses a dot grid paper rather than lined pages. Dot grid pages are a game-changer for me when it comes to note-taking. I'm no longer distracted by lines or restricted in the size of my handwriting. A dot grid is a great guide for handwriting notes in a straight line, but with the look of blank paper. If you haven't tried them before, give them a go and see if they work better for you than lined. I buy ring-bound A4 notepads in bulk from Amazon for my general notes. They are easy to work with and I can turn the page to landscape if required. They're helpful for drawing out tables and diagrams quickly, with the dots usually spaced to 0.5cm.

There's a whole Bullet Journal creative community online, sharing their "spreads", which is the whole design over two-facing pages. Some people go to great lengths and spend hours to get the aesthetic right. An immersive creative process, many use it to help their mental health and reduce anxiety. There are social media accounts created just around Bullet Journal spreads. They are stunning and I have huge handwriting envy.

I adore the concept and I'm looking forward to finally integrating it into my routine shortly. Bullet journaling may not look productive, but I view it as a creative outlet that happens to have a useful product at the end of the process. And for me, that also means potential new planner designs.

FORWARD PLANNING

I record almost everything in my planner. It's my go-to for everything going on in my life. The process of writing something down rather than typing it helps my brain process it differently. I've got over having to have it all looking perfect, which is just as well because I'm left-handed and have always struggled with neat writing. If my planner is full of scribbles, I know it's proving useful and worth my time drawing in the extra rows and columns that I need.

Using a coloured ink system keeps my brain interested and it is easier for me to use. I mark birthdays, anniversaries and any events I attend in red, as well as bills that are paid manually. Incoming money is in green, evening meals for each day are in blue, my weekly business checklist is in purple, housework tasks are in brown and general notes are in black, with other colours for various bits and pieces.

SCHOOL DATES

If you have children there's no getting away from the fact that everything is worked around school term dates, so it makes sense to get them in the diary first. You'll find them on your school website, so don't worry about any lost letters or sifting through emails.

Get all the term dates recorded. Look out for any sneaky inset days - they sometimes tag these on to bank holiday weekends, so at least there's some comfort in the fact you might get a chance to book a cheeky bonus weekend away. We've got Learning for Life days, where the kids have different lessons in the morning based on social topics such as relationships, drugs, mental health, etc. These days finish a couple of hours earlier and we have been caught out after forgetting them!

Check for any other dates on the school calendar, like parent's evenings, dress as a Unicorn Day (or whatever else the PTFA has come up with), non-uniform days and all those other days that most parents dread!

If they haven't got World Book Day marked down, a quick Google search will tell you when it is. Most schools participate but may not have it recorded on the school calendar yet. It's usually the first Thursday of March.

BIRTHDAY AND ANNIVERSARIES

Next, record birthdays and anniversaries and start to form some plans on how those days will look. Check whether they fall on a weekend or not. Our kids generally want sleepovers, so I always make note of the nearest Saturday to their birthdays.

If you remember, whenever the kids get an invite to a birthday party, record the date, or at least the nearest weekend for when their friend's birthdays are next year. They may not get invited again, but you'll know to look out for an invite and possibly have a plan for buying a gift and card well in advance.

HOLIDAYS AND TIME OFF

Next is whatever time off I want to book out, both for family breaks and time for myself. We may not know where we are going yet but we can still block the time out.

I tend to write my time away dates in green ink. Green is good, wholesome time well spent. It's time well needed and something positive to look forward to.

If I don't book time out like this, I can guarantee that it won't happen. I include one day off every four weeks for me and Ade to spend the day together. This is different from a normal day off, for us to get out and spend time with each other without the kids or anyone else. It is difficult with running two businesses without family support for respite. There's always the sick child curve-ball to put a spanner in the works too, so while every-thing is written down, it is always flexible. If we need to swap some days around, we do, but the intention to take time out is why it's written down on paper.

The problem with being too flexible though is that it sometimes leads to days off never happening. I've analysed our workflow in the fabrications company we run together and identified a few patterns throughout the year when it is possible to take time off without impacting too much on workflow and turnover. Summer is extremely busy, but this makes it even more impor-tant to book time off and stick to it. We make plans to increase productivity in the run-up to create some breathing space for taking most of August off.

GOOGLE CALENDAR

I'm very much a pen-and-paper person but using an online calendar is a fantastic addition to my planning, even more so now I've got more online calls to manage. I use Google Calendar because it's free, easy to use and tags onto my sidebar for a quick view when I'm working. It integrates well with other applications like Calendly (appointment booking software) and it's a useful organisation tool. I previously used Microsoft Outlook, which was a game-changer in getting life organised. I've downloaded the Google Calendar app and can check everything quickly on the go. Life has become a lot easier since embracing the online calendar. Mine is all colour coded, depending on what sort of activity I'm doing. I rely on it a lot right now but still work between that and my paper planner - the best of both worlds.

TIME BLOCKING

You may already be familiar with time blocking but if not, think back to your school timetable. There were set time slots each week to spend on lessons. The school organised this for you, with details on which classroom you were in and when. You'd refer to it until it was memorised, after which, you knew what you were doing on autopilot.

Except you're not at school anymore and you now oversee your own time. No one else tells you where you should be and at what time. You may feel resistance to this, particularly if one of the reasons you became self-employed was to free yourself from time constraints. You want to be flexible in your work, to mould it around your family or other commitments. You are your own boss, doing what you want when you want. That's how it goes, right?

If you want to succeed, then no. You also need to be disciplined with what you're doing and when. This forms part of your business strategy, looking at how much time you spend on tasks each week. It's too easy to become distracted at home - to wake in the morning not sure what you're working on today, to faff about and get nothing done, then repeat the same tomorrow because you have no structure in place on how best to focus your time and energy.

I was a stay-at-home mum during the mid to late nineties. I got involved in voluntary work setting up a new local community group. I made a lot of friends and gained valuable skills and experience that have helped me throughout my life.

I had postnatal depression with my firstborn and struggled to get through each day. When baby number two came along, I did everything I could to make sure it didn't happen again. I still got postnatal depression, but I found better ways of coping.

The first time around, I had almost no support network. As a young, single mum at nineteen, most of my friends were off out to the pub and I couldn't join them anymore. I lost most of my friends at that point.

I had no structure to my day and found myself struggling mentally to make it to bedtime each night. I worked harder to build a support network and daily structure the second time around. I made sure I was out and about, seeing people regularly for social visits and community work. There were meetings, fantastic networking days and all sorts of events going on. I thoroughly enjoyed that time of my life.

I kept myself physically fit walking everywhere with the buggy and would walk to the local leisure centre. They offered one free creche session a week, to be booked a week in advance. I'd go swimming and made it a rigid commitment every week. Everything I did was planned out.

I was here, there and everywhere! Realising I needed to get organised, I drew out a timetable for the week. I wrote in all the school runs, swimming, meetings, when I was seeing friends for a brew and when I was making tea. I think I even wrote what TV programmes I'd watch and when! I was time-blocking before time-blocking became a thing! I stayed on top of keeping the house straight and enjoyed renovating the garden, as well as looking after the kids and all my community work. Life was balanced, I thought.

However, if I saw a gap in my day, even a small one, I'd fill it. I feared having my depression get worse and thought that if I stopped to pause, it would hit me and I'd be back in the pit of despair that I'd struggled so hard to climb out of previously. I stayed busy and made sure I filled every minute of my day.

I didn't factor in any breathing space. Looking back now, some twenty-five years later, I'd created the habit of being busy. A few years later and juggling a difficult job, I was doing the same thing - cramming too much into my week. It was at that point I burned out for the first time, paying a heavy price and spending the best part of four years on the sofa with Chronic Fatigue whilst the rest of the world went by. To try and avoid depression, I'd put my physical health at risk, but I still got depression because my body wouldn't work properly. There were other contributing factors, but the main one was my not looking out for myself.

When blocking time for the week, always leave buffer time between the blocks or tasks. Having a structure is good, but make sure to leave gaps here and there. No back-to-back calls either. Make a brew and sit in the garden for a while. I spend time watching the birds here now we are semi-rural, as we get a good range of winged visitors. Read an article or blog – one that isn't work-related. Don't confuse this buffer time with dedicated self-care time that you should also be blocking out as a priority for each week, it is just some breathing time between tasks, to ground, restore, and then continue.

I've found the easiest way for me to keep track of my timetabled week is to print off the week on an A4 sheet and have it on a clipboard close to hand. It removes even having to find it on the computer. You can scrawl on it if things change, and you're not messing up your paper diary chopping and changing things around. You can download a PDF copy of mine via the QR code link at the back of the book. They're useful to file and keep as a reference should you want or need to audit your time to make things even more efficient.

TIME TRACKING

I worked for my local Fire and Rescue Service in Community Fire Safety, leaving in 2012. It was my last full-time employment role (barring a few part-time and agency posts). I worked on fire prevention in the community, with a reduction in domestic fires and fatalities as the focus.

For auditing purposes, we recorded our working day in minutes, which was 435 minutes for seven and a quarter hours. Submitting our timesheets monthly was a tedious job. We'd always forget to record daily and so spent the end of each month head-scratching and crying into the computer screen, promising ourselves we'd do it properly next month! It never happened though.

It wasn't so much to do with what hours we'd worked, but how we'd spent those 435 minutes. Different codes were used for different activities. We weren't supposed to be at our desks much, so if too much admin time was recorded, it was flagged.

This is a similar model to time tracking, recording what you're doing and when. I stumbled upon time tracking completely by accident in 2019. I was researching the Bullet Journal system discussed earlier in this chapter and ended up time tracking instead. It wasn't quite what I had planned, but it opened my eyes to where and how I was spending my time. I then realised it was similar to the time recording I'd done previously at the Fire Service.

It's a simple method. Write down your start time and what task you're working on. When you change the task, record the time on the next line and continue. Five-minute increments are detailed enough for this and you include whatever you want. Include things like breaks, if you go on social media, make a brew or get caught up sorting a load of washing.

This is a worthwhile exercise to understand where your time drains really are. It can become an intense task, so just do it over a couple of days at a time and schedule it in to repeat every quarter or whatever frequency suits you. At the end of each day, assess what you've done and when. Decide whether you are happy with how it looks.

Ask yourself the question, does it look like the schedule of a successful business owner? Are you spending your time on the right kind of tasks?

The big eye-opener for me was the time I'd spent doom-scrolling on social media. Be brutally honest with yourself for this exercise. You're not going to share this information with anyone unless you want to, it is just for you to get a better understanding of where your time is going. Throw your ego out of the window and make yourself accountable for how you're spending your time. If you think you're only on Facebook or Instagram for a quick ten minutes, then think again! It is so easy to lose half an hour and more falling down the rabbit holes.

When you get into the habit of writing down what and when, it becomes a lot easier. Keep your notepad within reach and in your line of sight so you don't forget.

Something else that happens when you track your time is that you instinctively become more aware of it. On the second day of tracking, I was already making improvements in being more efficient and focused on tasks. I'd become accountable to myself and didn't want to see at the end of the day that I'd wasted time on activities that didn't matter.

If you're going to give it a go, make it a thorough audit of how your time is spent. There are apps for this as well, if that's easier – Toggl is easy to use. I still prefer pen and paper, but whichever way you do it, it's a highly beneficial task.

Time tracking can also kickstart the building blocks of your daily and weekly business hours, and how long tasks take to do. This will help you to time block with confidence, so you're not just estimating the length of tasks.

HABITS

What springs to mind when you think of the word habits? Are we talking about giving up bad habits? Or creating new, positive ones?

Whichever way round, we'll benefit from making the change.

I visualise small habits as jigsaw puzzle pieces. If you think a small, seemingly insignificant change in your life won't have a huge impact, consider all those pieces put together and it becomes a much brighter picture. But establishing them all together would be overwhelming, and likely unsuccessful. When faced with overwhelm, break things down into small manageable microtasks. One step at a time is all that's required.

How do we create new habits? Or stop negative ones? Neuroplasticity is the official term. It is about growing new neural pathways in your brain and this is why it takes at least 21 days to form a new habit - possibly more depending on how receptive you are to making changes. I'm not a professional on this topic, but I can just about get my head around it. If we keep repeating new tasks or routines daily, that's when the pathways develop until we're then undertaking those tasks on autopilot. They've become a habit and the outcome we wanted. There are a lot of information sources online about Neuroplasticity if you want to read further on it.

We can help ourselves to be more successful in creating new habits by working on our motivation for change. Using the Five Ws and H method is a good start. A PDF worksheet is available via the QR code at the back of the book to help with this.

Ask yourself these questions:

- **WHAT** - ***what is the new habit you are wanting to create***? Write it down as an affirmation. The more specific this is, the more likely you'll succeed.
- **WHO** - ***who will benefit from this new habit?*** Yourself? Others? Whom does it impact and how? Who is affected by not creating the new habit?
- **WHY** - **why create this new habit?** Think about the outcome or reward. "If I create this new habit, the positive outcomes are . . .." this will help in motivating you to keep at it. Write them down so you can visualise those outcomes happening.
- **WHERE** - ***where will this new habit take place?*** Can you place visual cues to make sure you remember? For example, my little

medication tin is on my bedside table, left open so I can see whether my tablets are there or not. It's a visual cue so I know whether I've taken them or not. In over three years, I've only ever forgotten to do this once. I don't think that's bad going, although my motivation is extremely high – I don't want to end up back at the hospital! Another visual cue to use would be simple post-it notes within easy sight of where the habit usually takes place - at least as a temporary measure until the habit becomes established.

- **WHEN – *what time of day, and how often?*** Is it once a day or more? Weekly? Set an alarm on your phone. If you're a chronic alarm user, label all the alarms and give them different sounds. You'll soon get used to which sounds are prompt for a specific task without having to read what you're supposed to be doing.
- **HOW – *how can I make it easier to stick to this habit?*** Set alarms, move things around, swap things over. Placement of items can be all that is needed to make a habit more likely to stick. I've now put my overnight moisturiser in my bedside drawer so it's easier to reach once I've got into bed and realised I've forgotten to use it. That's better than going back to the

bathroom. My Apple watch gets charged on the tv unit where I know I can keep the charger plugged in. I walk past this in the morning so I'm less likely to forget to put my watch on. Having not worn a watch for the last thirty years, it's taken some time for it to stick.

HABIT STACKING

The concept of habit stacking is to introduce a new habit by attaching it to an already established task that might be similar or need to be done at the same time of day, or location. You start one task and after time, you'll flow to the task that's next without even thinking. An example is taking my herbs, which taste awful, so I always take them just before brushing my teeth. I do this without fail every morning and evening, taking the taste away.

Think about a factory production line. There are different jobs along the line to be done in a particular order. Or a line in a song - if you know the lyrics, each line is a prompt for the next and you sing along without thinking about it. Consider the times when you work on autopilot and you're in flow. Tasks get done one after the other without much thought. Do you always do tasks in the same sequence? Does each task immediately prompt the next? Yes? That's habit stacking. See if your stacks are already there. Is there anything else you can stack onto these? It's a great way to increase productivity without much extra thought.

MORNING ROUTINE

You don't have to be out of bed at 5 am to have a morning routine! I struggle to get out of bed most mornings, with fibromyalgia contributing to poor sleep and perimenopausal hormone fluctuations, but I still have a well-structured morning routine.

I have my morning routine tasks listed in my notes app, which I now only refer to if I feel I've forgotten something. It's a good way to work out your flow of tasks and a reminder when you first commit to making this habit stack part of your daily routine.

It doesn't matter what time your morning routine starts, it will serve you well. Here's what mine looks like:

- My alarm sounds. Adrian is already up with the kids and brings me a brew,
- Take medication (I need to take them before eating),
- Drink brew,
- Get dressed,

- Sort breakfast. I listen to podcasts whilst doing this,
- Make another brew,
- Take my herb supplements and brush my teeth,
- Wash my face, put makeup on if I'm wearing it that day,
- Sort my hair out,
- Faff around, open the blinds, switch the computer on,
- I'm ready for work!

It takes around an hour. Some days I'm so tired I go back to sleep, but when I get up, I still do all this in the same order, regardless of the time. It's a process that I need to perform to feel ready to start a working day. On the days this doesn't happen, I feel sluggish and demotivated, and I know it's down to not having my routine in place.

EVENING ROUTINE

My evening routine is a work in progress. I didn't think I needed one at first, but it's clear I do. It helps me to put in much-needed time boundaries. On the nights I don't follow this, I stay up late, watch rubbish TV, eat too late and then feel groggy and awful in the morning.

It impacts hugely on my day. It looks something like this:

- 19.00 teatime is finished, sit on the sofa, watch some TV with the youngest, chat about things,
- 20.00 No computer work after this. I watch something easy on tv for an hour, usually house/DIY programmes. I knit whilst watching,
- 21.00 go for a shower,
- 21.20 pj's on, moisturise, dry hair,
- 21.30 cup of tea, more TV and knitting,
- 22.00 bed.

This is what I'm working towards as a standard weekday evening. Sometimes it happens and sometimes it doesn't. It's difficult when you just want some time to yourself once the kids have gone to bed, but I know I benefit greatly from sticking to it and it makes life a lot easier. Knowing what to do and having the discipline to do it aren't necessarily the same thing!

It also helps me wind down - no computer work after 8 pm and a hot shower to help with fibro pains. I also sleep better knowing I've got clean hair and I don't have to shower in the morning, which takes longer. Morning Nic is always grateful whenever Evening Nic has completed her routine!

BATCHING TASKS

This is simply about completing tasks together, depending on what kind of work they are. It's easier to stick to one type of job for a while than to keep chopping and changing. Examples of this in a housework setting would be emptying all the bins at the same time, prepping food for the week and vacuuming all the rooms one after the other. It's to save time and energy by already being set up to do specific types of tasks. For business, you can batch emails, write newsletters in one sitting and create multiple Canva graphics instead of just one or two when needed, thus creating time efficiency, ease and flow. If you think it's not worth using batching, consider how long it would take to iron clothes only as you need them, even more so if you already do this. You get the ironing board out, wrestle to put it up, get the iron, fill it with water, iron your outfit, switch the iron off, empty it, put it away, and put the board away.

That's a lot of faff for one outfit that's likely to get worn once before going in the wash. There are two answers to solve that problem – batch iron your clothes, or don't iron! Either is acceptable.

To round off this chapter, the tasks you can look at undertaking are:

1. Populate your planner/diary. Whether a physical or digital version, use colour coding to help identify your different activities.
2. Use a time block sheet to help with planning out your week.
3. Have a go at time tracking for a couple of days each month or quarter. Find out where you're really spending your time and make some changes if necessary.
4. Identify your motivation for creating a new habit. Use the five W/H PDF printout.
5. Consider habit stacking. Identify where you are already doing this and see if you can incorporate any new habits.
6. If you don't already have them, create a morning and evening routine to help start and box off the day.

PDF worksheets to help with some of these tasks are available via the QR code in the back of the book.

Chapter 3

Efficiency - Business Owners Edition

When you step into the role of a business owner, the focus is generally on how to become efficient in business. But there's so much to do that it becomes overwhelming and tasks start to get pushed to one side.

We strive to discover better ways of working and discover a wide range of business support out there to help with business growth, freeing up precious time, instead of you learning and doing everything yourself. You work towards outsourcing tasks like website design or email management. You learn as you go, becoming more efficient as time goes by.

Home life often takes a hit as you switch your focus. The mess mounts up, stuff is no longer tidied away and mealtimes become an inconvenience. The more you immerse yourself into your business, the less time is available to keep on top of running your home.

What if we were able to prepare our homes before this stage? What if we saw streamlining our homes and lives as an essential part of preparing to become business owners? Would this be a reasonable task to undertake? I'd say so.

But many business owners don't have a planned exit strategy to leave employment or consider how it will fully affect dynamics at home. Perhaps only focusing on the positive aspects of working from home means the problems it also raises are easily overlooked. Being able to work in your pyjamas or not having a bullying boss aren't good enough reasons on their own, we also need a purpose and a wider mission - something to work towards.

YOUR BIG WHY

The meaning of life. Your life. Why you're in business. *This* business. Until you get clear on this, you'll go around in circles, chasing shiny objects that take your focus away from the main objective. "To make money" might not be enough of a motivator to fully invest your heart and soul in your business. Your why needs to evoke strong emotions as your motivation driver. One of the main reasons people choose to create their own business is freedom and flexibility - to not be told by others when to go to work, when to go home, what time to eat lunch etc., and to have more control over their time and how they spend it.

If you want to dig more into your why, I recommend the book "Start With Why" by Simon Sinek. He nails it. Work out your why and it'll save you years of head-scratching. It's all about your purpose, your bigger mission and what you're really selling - which might not be what you think at first glance.

STATIONERY ISSUES

If you've found yourself drawn to entrepreneurship, it's likely that your brain comes up with new ideas every single day. You find inspiration in the smallest of details and the strangest of places. I've got a small notebook filled with post-it notes on all the bigger ideas I've had that are future projects to investigate.

How do you deal with all your ideas? Do you remember half of them? You need a simple system to capture these thoughts and bank them.

I've lost count of the number of notebooks I have from the last ten years, all stuffed full of ideas that could be turned into successful business projects. What I wanted to focus on was finding a way to capture these ideas as soon as they pop into my head. For too long, my ideas were dismissed by those around me as rubbish, nonsense, never going to work, etc. It's only in the last ten years I've started to write things down, started to truly believe in myself and to know that whilst the idea may not be feasible right now, it's worth parking and percolating over. It's worth saving to revisit later with fresh eyes and thoughts on it.

As technology improves, so does the way we can record and store things. I haven't invested in a Remarkable writing tablet, but I have heard good things about them and seen them in use. They seem easy to use and clearly take up a lot less space than 20 notebooks.

My problem is that I'm still a traditional pen-and-paper person. I love the feel of a new notebook, with fresh pages to write on. I'm not sure that feeling will ever go away. I'm a visual creative. I love to write and doodle. I've tried storing ideas on my phone or computer, and it doesn't feel the same for me.

I've ordered duplicates of the same notebook, but all this did was confuse me. I had no dedicated note-books for specific ideas, so I've turned to buying different themed notebooks and using them for each kind of idea. This is a must now for me and gives me the perfect excuse to buy a new notebook! At the time of writing, I've got around five major projects I'm working on and I'm keeping those notes organised and segregated from the rest so they're easy to find.

DIGITAL CAPTURE

Digital technology is arguably a more streamlined option. I rely heavily on the Notes app on my phone when I'm out and about without a notebook. My iPhone lets me pin notes to the top of the list, so my regular lists and notes are always easy to find. These currently look like this:

- Medication – to record dosage times,
- Weekly meal plan,
- Grocery shop – for items we don't tend to buy every week to be added to the next order,
- General errands – for when I'm out and about,
- Birthdays – dates and potential gift ideas for the coming year,
- Christmas – for ideas and purchases,
- Amazon shopping list – for personal and business. Unless it's urgent, I group items to buy together, to save on packing and delivery

trips (we have Prime, so delivery cost isn't the main factor),

- Running task list – making appointments, returning orders, making phone calls etc.,
- Morning routine,
- Evening routine.

For taking notes on the go or when I'm just throwing ideas around, I'll sometimes press record and video myself chattering away when I'm in flow with new ideas. I'll put them through a transcription app, such as Otter.ai, to turn my ramblings into text. The dictation mode in Microsoft Word works well too.

BRAIN DUMPS AND EUREKA MOMENTS

Dedicate some time each week to daydream and let your ideas flow. If you are going to carve this time out each week, make sure you've curated your environment for creative flow. This could be going for a long soak in the bath, going for a walk, sitting in the garden, putting some of your favourite tunes on, listening to some inspiring podcasts or meditating. I find a lot of ideas flow when I'm walking by the sea. I always take notebooks and pens with me whenever we're away for a few days.

GOAL SETTING

We've been set goals throughout our lives. At school, the goals are to pass our exams. Many of us will aim to pass our driving test. Having a framework to help us build our goals stops us from wandering aimlessly with no direction. The SMART framework is a renowned and useful tool used for goal setting.

When considering setting yourself a goal, the goal must be:

- Specific - Be specific in your intentions. Set a distinctive goal with attention to detail,
- Measurable - how are you going to tell whether you're achieved the goal or not? Add some direct numbers or figures into the equation,
- Achievable - the goal needs to be within your skill level, or that you are able to learn the skills to make it feasible,
- Realistic - becoming an astronaut isn't going to be particularly realistic for most of us... neither is becoming a billionaire, for that matter. Get realistic with your facts and figures,
- Timely - attach a timeframe to your goal, otherwise, it'll never be urgent enough to work on.

Make sure the goals you set are yours and not the expectations of others. They need to come from the heart and be put into place for the right reasons.

ACCOMPLISHMENT

For a long time, I couldn't identify what would make me feel like I was doing enough to build my business. I stumbled upon a podcast by Carrie Green of the Female Entrepreneur Association, where she used the word *accomplished*. It was the exact word I'd been searching for and I now use it as my daily focus. Do I feel accomplished today? Have I done enough?

I'd struggle to settle in an evening if I didn't feel accomplished - like I hadn't earned my sleep. I've had to develop my mindset on this. On days when I feel like I've not done enough, I look closer at what I have done. Sometimes, smaller tasks can often be larger milestones on our journey. We can get them ticked off as milestones towards the bigger goals. Once I started to think this way, I felt more content in my day-to-day work. I can always see progress, even on days that don't go to plan. I've reframed fibro flare days to me letting my body have what it needs, which is rest and recuperation. I feel more content and although it does still happen occasionally, overwhelm and frustration are thankfully infrequent emotions.

MOTIVATION

What kind of motivation do you need? Is money part of it? Maybe it's not related to finances. It might be to create a business that gives you the flexibility to take time off during school holidays or a goal that is based on helping a certain number of people. Motivators are different for everyone and they can be the difference between getting out of bed and staying there. Consider what gets you out of bed every morning and whether your motivation needs some help.

I have a printout of what I'd consider our dream home to look like stuck on the wall by my bed. I look at it every morning in the hope it helps me get my backside out of bed. It's not working though, so I'll be putting up a cork noticeboard and creating a vision board purely based on motivating me to get up. I'll make sure to change it up regularly too. It's important to do this or it'll just blend into the background with everything else.

Stick quotes and pictures around your home as a constant reminder of why you're doing all of this. Put them in your line of sight everywhere you can think of. Inside your kitchen cupboard door where you keep the tea and coffee, so each time you go to make a brew you get a reminder of your awesomeness as a business owner. Keep them fresh and relevant. See how you get on with using these, alongside any other visual reminders you can use to stay motivated and on track.

ACCOUNTABILITY

Setting a goal isn't always enough. Many people also need some form of accountability to achieve their goals, knowing full well that if no one is checking up on them, they'll waste weeks, months, or even years faffing about, putting things off and moving deadlines because they can, with no one to tell them otherwise. I can relate to this because I did it myself.

I now work better with hard deadlines and bigger projects, so people know what I'm doing, and when. I've made my deadlines become non-negotiable. I focus on what's on the other side of the task ahead of me and what will happen when I reach the goal or complete the project. I know that if I want to uplevel, I need to do the work.

There are different ways to make this happen for yourself. Accountability buddies in online networking groups are a good start but you need to think about who you're letting down if you don't reach the goals that you set.

What's the penalty for not reaching your target? Is this enough to get you to do the work?

I've created my own hard deadline right here with this book. The launch date was agreed upon, with everything scheduled around it. It hasn't been an easy process, we've had some awful things happen between my committing to writing the book and launch day, and it's affected work dramatically, but my only other option was not to launch. This book is also a huge life goal for me and I'd be letting myself down immensely by not finishing it. Having let lots of people know, I don't want to be that person that doesn't follow through on promises to herself. I've done enough of that already and being brutally honest with myself, I've run out of excuses.

Another way of working with accountability is joining a business hive mind or peer mentoring group. These are for keeping each other motivated and accountable, getting feedback on your ideas, and potential work collaborations. The vibe is different from larger networking groups, they're a more intimate setting. A lot of these are substantial financial investments, so participants will want to get the best out of them.

You're more likely to show up for yourselves and others. You can set up your own for free, but from experience,

I've found that it's a lot easier to show up when there's skin in the game, as opposed to a friendly agreement.

BODY DOUBLING

This is a popular discussion topic within online neurodiverse communities. The theory is you'll get more done when you're working alongside someone else, rather than trying to motivate yourself when you're on your own. It's not about feeling shame for not doing anything, it's about having someone with you and mirroring the other person who is working. You motivate each other and keep each other accountable. If you find it impossible to start work on your own, this is the method for you.

If we're working from home on our own, it can become tedious. You get distracted and bored. This is where working in an office with others seems a lot more appealing. You motivate each other, stop for a quick chat and a brew, and then get back on with work. But working from home alone is very different. You might have dogs or cats for company, but it's not quite the same! We still need connection with others to keep going.

Online co-working sessions are a feasible way to create a community office-style environment. Someone arranges a time, invites everyone to what's most likely a Zoom call, people log in and say what they're going to work on in the time allotted, which may be a couple of hours in length. Everyone then turns their microphone off and gets on with their work.

Think of it as Big Brother watching you! Okay, you could be doing your nails for all they know, and not working on the sale page you'd declared you were doing, but it is helpful to know that these exist, and if you know you don't work without company, they are essential.

You can find accountability pods within some social media groups. They're usually via paid monthly membership subscriptions with various business coaches and mentors. If you aren't aware of any, start with local networking groups, and take it from there. If you still can't find any that are your vibe, create your own!

BE YOUR OWN DEADLINE DOMINATRIX

Have I just invented a thing? I daren't Google to check.

I recall submitting assignments at University with around fifteen minutes to spare. The penalty for late submission was a percentage deduction of your mark, yet I'd be faffing around until the last 48 hours before the deadline, when hyperfocus mode magically appeared. Up until recently, I viewed myself as a methodical worker - an organised person who did the work upfront. I wasn't a deadline dancer; I didn't need hard stops to get my work done.

Except I do need hard deadlines! Since switching my mindset and creating better accountability for myself, my productivity has increased massively. But this has only come about because I've tried several different approaches and have only just started to find the ones that work well for me.

When we work for ourselves, it really is too easy not to do the work. We need to put strict boundaries in place to see the results. This may sound counter-intuitive if you have left corporate environments due to restrictions placed upon you. You want freedom and flexibility by working for yourself, so you may not want or think you need structures and boundaries in place. This couldn't be further from the truth and to succeed, it's imperative that you have them.

STRATEGY AND SYSTEMS

If I started talking about strategies and systems to you, what comes to mind first? Maybe stuff like workflow processes, KPIs, SOPs, software systems and networks.

Do they sound boring? Yes. Are they essential to business success? Also, yes. Without a framework to work within, how do you know that what you're doing is taking you in the right direction? For years, I plodded along, living in hope that one day, everything would slot into place and it'd all come good. In recent years, I've realised I was missing a huge part of the puzzle. I needed a business strategy to get me to where I wanted to be.

You may have jumped into entrepreneurship headfirst, with no warning or plan. Suddenly, you're doing the job of 20 people, all with different skills. And you're also working from home, which still needs running effectively. How do you get everything working together?

A strategy is simply setting out what you want to achieve and how you're going to achieve it. Back to goal setting, I guess, setting it out properly, with timescales and what you're going to sell. Without going into too much detail here (because strategy, as well as time management, are books all on their own), a general way of rounding it up would be:

- Decide how much money you want to make,
- When you want to make it by,
- What you're going to sell to make that amount of money, in that amount of time,

- How you're going to sell the things,
- How you're going to find your customers,
- Project manage all of this to make it happen, with milestones along the way, measuring your progress and creating forecasts to stay on track.

There's clearly a lot more detail involved but that's a basic overview of what a business strategy could look like. Without one, it's going to be a lot harder and take longer. It helps with motivation and procrastination and gives you a clearer path to where you want to be in twelve months. Strategy can be split up and mapped out over different periods of time – three, six, twelve months, three and five years, etc. Begin with the end goal, and work backwards from that. Work out how you're going to get there, create your plan and go for it.

CEO HEAD – BECOMING YOUR OWN BOSS

It's time to develop a serious business head. If you can get your head around it, you need to think and act like a CEO and treat yourself like an employee. Be the boss to yourself that you wish you'd always had, firm but fair. This isn't about being mean but it is about putting some firm boundaries in about how you'll work.

You might be wondering what this has to do with becoming more organised. What I've come to realise is that the sooner we create a CEO mindset for ourselves, the sooner we look at how we can run our businesses more efficiently. We make better decisions, we save time and money.

CREATE YOUR OWN EMPLOYMENT CONTRACT

If you were employed by someone else, you'd have a contract that would have to comply with employment law, which is in place to:

- ensure a healthy and safe working environment,
- ensure employees get adequate breaks,
- clarify where everyone stands regarding holiday and sick pay,
- ensure a minimum working wage and any overtime enhancements,
- ensure a maximum hourly working week,
- protect from bullying and harassment in the workplace,
- ensure suitable training for the role expected,
- provide suitable PPE if required, a comfortable working environment, access to fresh air and light, etc.

How many of the above do you consider when working for yourself?

You'd also undertake regular training, sign to say you've read and understood various policies and procedures and pay due care and attention to your own safety, to avoid accidents.

Would you work for someone if they didn't offer paid holidays? Or sick pay? What about if they expected you to work twelve-hour days with minimal breaks? What if they expected you to work even though your kids were sick and needed collecting from school? Who would work for an employer like that? Would they even get away with those terms and conditions?

The short answer is no. But when we work for ourselves, a lot of us put ourselves in these situations. We don't allow ourselves healthy working conditions.

Why do we expect that we can just carry on working regardless? It's a messy scenario. On one hand, we want to build our businesses, on the other, we need a healthy balance in life, a decent hourly rate and a boss that's understanding. But if we're not providing that for ourselves, then we've just agreed to unacceptable working conditions. If we had staff and treated them in this way, we'd end up with complaints, no workforce and a potential tribunal.

Your employment contract can be as simple as an A4 bullet-pointed sheet, committing to what you will and won't do. Pin it up where you can see it, near where you normally work so you can see it daily. State how many hours you will work per day, with a weekly maximum, whether you'll work weekends or not, when you'll take breaks, what you'll do when you or the kids are unwell etc. You could create a dress code for yourself, like no working in yoga pants or slippers. Whatever you feel would work for you. It won't take long to put together, an hour at most. Change it up if it's not working, but try and commit to it for three months, then review it and see if it's still fit for purpose.

It's another part of removing some of the mental load and clearing a bit more headspace, having your own policies and procedures in place for scenarios that may occur. Put your employment contract together when you're not feeling rushed. Take some time to think about how you want to work and what expectations you have of yourself. Be realistic about it and see it as starting to put some boundaries into place for yourself.

YOUR HOURLY RATE

You may want to consider creating an hourly rate for the work you put in. This will help a lot in deciding how and when to outsource. An example would be that you value your hourly working rate at £50 per hour. If it takes you ten hours to write a sales page, that's £500. If you ask a copywriter or VA to do it, you may be paying them the same £50 per hour, but it only takes them two hours to do the work. This is the perfect example of when to outsource when funds allow.

OUTSOURCING

One of the best pieces of advice I've been given is to outsource before you're ready. This can be difficult when funds are tight, so look at what the immediate problem is in front of you. What's causing a bottleneck in your work? What is stopping you from progressing? This could be that you don't have a sign-up page for people to join your email list, or that you need to invest in a software package to create graphics, such as the paid version of Canva. It's at this point you make the decision whether to spend or not. Is spending that money going to give you a quicker return on investment than waiting and struggling? Only you can make that call.

GAMIFICATION

For years I held a secret, one I was ashamed of because I didn't think anyone would take me seriously. I felt like a bit of a joke and questioned my sanity at times.

During my twenties, I'd play life out as a video game in my head. I lost days on end playing *Legend of Zelda* and *Super Mario* in my mid to late teens. My brain loved the fact you could be someone else in these virtual worlds and go about your business, completing random quests, collecting items and working out how to get to the next level.

I drew upon this way of thinking every time life got more difficult. I put my Zelda hat on and got through the day by telling myself to complete specific tasks. If I managed to do them, I got enough points to move to tomorrow, where new quests were waiting.

I wasn't totally obsessed with this way of thinking, but it cropped up a lot when I needed to ground myself to get motivated or to work through a difficult situation. I used it as a tool to get me through tough days but would never have admitted it to anyone like I am now.

Sound ridiculous? Stay with me!

A couple of years ago, I started to see the word gamification pop up in my news feeds on social media. I didn't take much notice at first, but as the topic came nearer to the surface, I started to investigate and I was amazed at what I saw.

For those who aren't familiar with the term, it is as follows (according to Wikipedia):

> ***"Gamification is the strategic attempt to enhance systems, services, organisations and activities by creating similar experiences to those experienced when playing games to motivate and engage users. This is generally accomplished through the application of game-design elements and game principles in non-game contexts."***

It made total sense to me. I hadn't been ridiculous, I was just using a tool that's proven to work - to gamify tasks to make them more achievable.

When I see gamification discussed online, it's in the context of business - offering points for people who complete specific training or sell the most tickets to an event. You see it a lot in online challenges on social media. A pop-up group that's doing a three-day challenge may offer prizes to everyone who participates in the challenge every day, or who is seen to be the biggest community cheerleader. These prizes are offered to encourage the community aspect, as well as help with engagement to increase visibility. It's a great motivator for those who like to win or have a competitive streak.

But what about in the context of running your home? Can we use it for that? The answer is, yes, because I've done it. Many of you are probably already doing this but don't realise it. How many times have you said to yourself "I've only got twenty minutes, let's see how much I can get done in that time?" That's gamification. You challenge yourself to get as much done as possible. Does it work for you? Are you giving yourself a small reward at the end?

Using this method might increase your productivity, help you work more efficiently and give you a sense of accomplishment, which, for me, is the best feeling. If I feel accomplished, I sleep better.

How could you use this to your advantage? It can be a good motivator for tidying up with younger children – challenge them to be the first one to fill a box or basket with toys. Ask them to go find specific items around the house and bring them back to you – incorporate this into sorting particular types of items. Reward charts for kids? Gamification. It was there under our noses all along.

To round off this chapter, the tasks to consider undertaking are:

1. Identifying your big why. Dig deep to find the reasons why you're invested in building this business.
2. Work out systems (physical and digital) to capture your ideas and store them so you don't lose them. Work out how best to arrange or organise them to suit you.
3. Set some goals using the SMART framework.
4. Create a vision board to help with motivation and your goal-setting.

5. Find an accountability pod or online co-working group or membership that you could join.
6. Look at whether you've got a business strategy in place. If you need help creating one, there are a lot of coaches and mentors that can help you.
7. Create your own employment contract.
8. Think of where you already use gamification in your life. See if there's anywhere else you can use it to improve your productivity.

Chapter 4

Living At Work – Perks And Pitfalls

If you work from home, this is, in part, what you're doing. You're running a business in a space designed mostly to live in, not work in. Working from home has increased now to the point where newer homes tend to incorporate a small spare room or study. But, if you need it as a bedroom, then you're a bit scuppered for a space you can close off to the rest of the house. House footprints are generally smaller too. Even without working from home, we are having to squeeze our living environments into smaller spaces.

What do workspaces look like at home? There's no definitive answer as it's different for everyone. I used to live in a four-bedroomed house, with an additional office.

I had a choice of rooms for my office and workroom. The house did eventually need to become a five-bedroomed property. We now reside in a four-bedroomed townhouse over three floors, with all bedrooms occupied.

My "office" is an alcove section of the lounge, giving the illusion (to anyone on a Zoom call) that I have a separate office to work from without interruption. This couldn't be further from the truth. In my line of sight ahead of me, between my computer monitors, is the TV in the corner. To my right are a pair of Juliet balcony doors that I can't open properly because there's a small filing cabinet there that won't fit anywhere else right now. It's distracting when people go past and I'm glad we live in a cul-de-sac otherwise it would be impossible to work.

TEMPORARY WORKSTATIONS

Having a separate office at home makes it far easier to switch off from work by just shutting the door and keeping it closed from the rest of the home. Even if you don't have a dedicated workroom, there are things you can do to make the transition easier from work mode to home living mode. Some of this can be aided with storage solutions and how you make use of the space when you need it to perform as a workspace, rather than a home space.

I work on the computer most of the time, at my desk, with files and notebooks behind me on bookcase shelves, but at one point, I was painting furniture on the kitchen table and running out of room every day, shifting all my work for everyone to eat at the table in the evening and then moving everything back when the evening meal was done. I didn't want to eat in front of the TV unless it was takeaway on a Saturday evening. It wasn't ideal, but it was all I could do at the time.

I resented the extra time and energy spent moving stuff around and yearned for a space where I could fully express my creativity and build my business.

I finally found a workshop near home, and then a retail shop. For various reasons, this didn't work out. I ended up renting a storage container and continued with my furniture painting commissions back where I started on the kitchen table, only I was much busier now. I was still running a concession stall at a local antique centre, so I continued to create items for sale.

It's important to be realistic about the practicalities of what kind of work can be done from home. There's a whole army of furniture painters, their homes stacked with raw projects awaiting renovation, works in progress and finished pieces, waiting to be sold. Many have workshops or build workrooms in their gardens. But for those that don't, they often end up living in what looks like a furniture warehouse. I know because I've done it and it's not ideal.

If you don't have a dedicated workspace, there are things you can do to make the space work better, without compromising home comforts.

If you need to create a temporary desk space at the kitchen table which needs moving for mealtimes, have a bag or storage basket with your desk items in, and any other things you need to be able to set up for the day - laptop, notebooks, pens, phone, files, folders, hole punch, stapler etc. Make it part of your going-to-work routine by laying everything out ready to use, which should only take five minutes. Lay out a cutting mat or desktop mat as a visual cue that whilst this is laid down on the table, it's your work desk.

When it's packed away, the space becomes the family dining table again. This doubles up as a visual cue and process to say you have finished work for the day.

Look to create visual transitions to help your brain shift from work to home mode - even something simple like a photo frame with some affirmations in it. Add that to your work bag/basket to put out whilst working. There are lots of little ideas you could incorporate. Have a think and see what you've got available.

If you need to use the kitchen table as a crafting work-bench, I've found that for smaller craft projects, having different trays for different projects works well. Visualise the large trolleys in school or work canteens where everyone puts their dirty trays ready to clean up. The nearest I can find to this type of storage is the Ikea Trofast system. I'll talk about that more in the Ikea section coming up.

Smaller, three-tier portable trolleys are useful for housing items that need regular moving around. Some of them have a removable wooden top, so you can use them as side tables too.

When I think about temporary workspaces in the home, I always look at how I can use furniture better. Our desks at home are doubled up back-to-back. They are two older desktops bought from a local nursery that was closing. They straddle a pair of 2x4 cube Kallax units from Ikea. It doesn't look perfect, but it works well. The best bit? Our grandchildren love hiding under-neath and using it as a den, crawling through the Kallax bottom shelves as part of the adventure. It takes up a lot of room in our lounge, but to be honest, we wouldn't be using that space for anything else right now.

MILLIMETRE PERFECT STORAGE

I can't help but recommend Ikea for making the most of smaller space living. There's a wide range of furniture in the exact dimensions you require, with different styles, colours and designs.

I reworked my office space recently. My blue-painted sideboard was becoming a bit cluttered and battered. I didn't have enough floor space for my office chair so, after a quick measure-up, I started planning how many Ikea Billy Bookcases I could get in the space.

I'd gone for the deeper bookcases because I need them to house the larger lever arch files that I use for our fabrications company. I planned out the space, ordered and paid online, and was able to collect them the next day. A great tip is to book the click-and-collect service. This solves three problems:

- You don't want to pay delivery charges,
- The items aren't available for delivery,
- You can't bear to go around the shop because you'll lose three days out of your life that you'll never get back.

They'll have all your items waiting for you on a trolley and the click-and-collect desk is near the exit. It was the perfect streamlined solution as we needed them quickly and couldn't get the deeper shelf ones delivered.

I've got almost floor-to-ceiling storage now, which is a huge bonus in a rental property as we have restrictions on what we can attach to the wall. Everything is easier to find, whether that's my crafting items, stationery, or business items such as files, folders, hole punches, staplers, post-its, etc. The printer is housed just behind me on a lower shelf, and with adjustable height shelving allowing accommodation of all my other books, storage boxes, and everything else. It's been a great changeover. I've made the best use of the space and none of it is crowded. It's my happy little corner of our home where I keep all my bits and pieces!

It means that everything is now off the floor, so no more moving random items to vacuum. Everything is compartmentalised and given a specific place on the shelves. If it does start to get a bit messy, it's easy to do a quick reset by making sure everything is put back where it's supposed to be. Everything has a home, and there's nothing on the shelves that shouldn't be there.

What I love about Ikea is when they list furniture dimensions, they are exact. You know what you're getting. The quality is good enough to not fall apart.

You can measure the space and plan out perfectly how things will fit. I've yet to be stuck with not finding the right type of storage or furniture solution from Ikea.

With versatile ways to use the furniture, their website shows a range of finished rooms, including real-life setups from happy customers. There's been a lot of thought given to how items are used and where they might be placed in the home.

IKEA STORAGE STAPLES

My favourite functional ranges, as a happy Ikea customer for the last 30 years, are as follows:

Billy Bookcase - With two different depth options and various widths and heights, a combination of wider and narrower ones has been the perfect solution for us. The narrower bookcases are the perfect width to house four large lever arch files, with just enough wiggle room to grab them easily without them getting stuck.

Malm Bedroom Furniture - There are various pieces in the range, consisting mainly of different sizes of drawer sets. Whichever colour you choose, it gives you a streamlined, almost fitted-furniture look. With beds and dressing tables to match, they go well with some of the other furniture ranges. They repaint and upcycle well for a different look. The drawers are strong and sturdy, I've had some now for over ten years and they still look great.

Pax Wardrobe System – These have a seemingly endless range of interior fittings and are truly versatile systems that you design for your needs. If you need longer hanging space or extra shelves, it's feasible. You can buy internal drawer systems individually. If you're on a budget and can't afford to buy everything straight-away, just buy the carcass and doors and then add the interior fittings as and when you can manage.

With hanging rails, slide-out rails, trouser rails, jewellery drawers and other compartments galore, a selection of door styles, with traditional openers or sliding doors, everything is interchangeable and adaptable. I've seen the Pax wardrobe units used in kitchens, with the doors left off and the internal drawers and shelves used as display units. A truly versatile storage system for any room in the home.

Trofast – An open drawer system with different depths of plastic trays or drawers. Generally marketed for children's bedrooms, they are a useful bit of kit for craft rooms, recycling stations, garage storage, under the stairs, and utility rooms. The plastic trays are easy to clean and available in different colours.

Kallax - the cube lover's delight! Based around square modular shelving. Available in individual cubes and units including formations of 1x2, 2x2, 3x4, 4x4, and 5x5 cube shelves that can also become a room divider if fixed in place.

There are so many more storage systems available depending on budget. The ones I've included work out better value than other ranges. They make the best use of space and can be used in any room of the home. Look on the Ikea website for inspiration on how you could use them. What storage problems could they solve for you?

UTILISING OLDER FURNITURE

When I ran my previous business, painting and renovating furniture, I came across all sorts of furniture designs and styles, including an old 1950s writing bureau with glass cabinets on either side. The veneer had come away in places and it did look scruffy. I could see the potential and knew that once painted, it would make a fantastic statement piece.

I used it at home for a while before renovating it. The drop-down leaf of the bureau was the perfect size to use my laptop. There were the usual smaller storage compartments inside, originally designed for writing paper and envelopes. They were the perfect size for pen storage and smaller notebooks. I used the top of the unit as a shelf for books, and there were three drawers underneath for smaller craft items. There was a lot of storage in one piece of furniture and the best part of it was the glass display cabinets on either side. Originally designed to display your great granny's old bone china tea set, I found they were the perfect size for all my A4 files and folders. I couldn't have planned it better.

After six months, I renovated and sold it. Unfortunately, I hadn't realised just how much stuff it had housed. It took me a good while to find homes for all the displaced items and part of me wishes I'd not parted with it.

I had another smaller bureau, a lovely functional little piece. I was surprised it didn't sell straight away and it was one of the pieces I still had when we finally closed our final concession stall. I'm glad to say we still have it in a small alcove in our hallway and we love it. It houses the dog leads, poo bags, emergency tape measure, emergency pens and pencils and a few other bits and pieces. The one drawer underneath has the shoe polish tin, and a couple of catalogues There's room underneath to keep shoes out of the way temporarily and it's just a lovely little piece of furniture that's decorative and functional - the perfect-sized piece for a small alcove.

Another project I had was a Lebus tallboy. This is one of the most useful items I've owned. It was never put up for sale because the inside of the cupboard kept messing up when I painted it. It's now part of our hallway storage and is filled with paints, messier craft items and all sorts of bits and pieces. The cupboard part has two very generous shelves. There are two drawers in the base and the top of the unit lifts up to reveal a mirror on the inside of the lid and a shallow storage tray with different compartments. We keep stuff like head torches, tape and other emergency bits and pieces here. The drawers have paintbrushes and sundries in one and heat pads and hot water bottles in the other.

I ended up renovating and repainting a lot of bureau or secretaire pieces. They are vintage hidden gems as far as storage solutions go. With a range of different shapes and sizes, it's worth hunting around to find a piece the right size for your needs.

Don't be put off by utilising older furniture pieces, thinking they are past their use. By giving them a new lease of life with a colourful renovation, they can be a useful and stylish addition. A mix of old and modern is a great balance for creating a functional and comfortable home.

PORTABLE RECORDING STUDIOS

At the time of writing, I don't have a published podcast, but I do have one planned. Am I looking at a professional studio for recording? No! I'm using a fabric-covered three-fold tabletop presentation screen.

Accidentally bought in 2019 from the local auction house, it was our first time trying their online bidding service. I'm not sure what happened, but the sale confirmation came through and it cost me about £12.

Despite my error, it has turned out to be an extremely useful item. Used as a toilet cubicle for when grandchildren are potty training and need privacy, it's a perfect solution. It also gets used regularly as part of den building and whatever else they're playing. It's been used at our Amateur Dramatics group to cordon off the Musical Director playing the keyboard during performances and I use it regularly to set out ideas with post-it notes when I want to plan something out.

We use it to blank off the Juliet balcony windows to stop the dogs barking at passers-by and I've recently set it up and tried it out on my other desk as a podcast booth, with a blanket folded across the top and me standing in front of it. I've trialled it a few times and it's helped a lot in improving the sound quality when recording. When I'm done, it folds down and slots under the desk.

You don't need a professional setup to get started - just some creative thinking and a willingness to try things out. This will suit me perfectly until I reach a point where I might need a professional studio.

Have a look around your home and see what you've got that could help you with similar work tasks. Use blank wall spaces for face-to-camera videos, or wall hangings in your brand colours. One of my business coaches installed a roller blind on the wall in their office that was only used when recording face-to-camera video. It made the perfect backdrop in her branding colours. The rest of the time it was rolled up and out of the way. Is something like this feasible anywhere in your home?

ALTERNATIVE STORAGE SOLUTIONS

Since closing the shop and concession stalls, I've still got some display pieces that I can't bear to part with. One of them is Delilah, a female torso mannequin. She houses my beaded necklaces and summer hats. I love the fact she's decorative *and* useful. I also use her to stage and photograph handmade jewellery and hand-knitted scarves for Etsy. She's a multi-functional piece who earns her keep.

Next to Delilah is an old painted wooden ladder, leaning against the wall to house my scarf collection. I wear a lot of scarves in winter and it's easy to just grab one from there, rather than root around in my wardrobe.

Although I try to keep most of the house streamlined for ease, I'm a Maximalist at heart. I love things out on display. For the moment, it's not practical to have the entire house filled with pieces like this, but with a few here and there for inspiration, they're a little bit of motivation to keep working toward our forever home.

My pen and pencil collections are on my bookshelves in my office space. None of them are packed away in drawers, they're all in pots. I've got small studio pottery vases and planters, mugs that are chipped or those odd-shaped gift ones that don't fit in the cupboard with the rest of them. I've decorated an old pine utensil storage block to house paintbrushes and my ruler collection (yes, I have a ruler collection).

Glass jars and nicely shaped glass bottles are full of seed beads of different colours and sizes, so whilst they're awaiting transformation into bespoke jewellery, I can enjoy them as stunning jewelled displays. I have countertop acrylic shop display columns turned upside down to house wallpaper rolls for crafting and decoupage and various sturdy gift boxes to house smaller items. A cylindrical, painted bottle box houses my knitting needles. I don't see the point in buying storage like this when you can use what you already have. I take far greater pleasure in upcycling and repurposing. Once a creative, always a creative.

Can you make use of things you've already got? Look for hooks, racks or rails to hang jewellery, scarves and hats. Sort through your mugs and any that are chipped or just plain awkward in shape, pull them out and use them as pen pots. I challenge you to find five small items you can repurpose into quirky, useful storage. I could write an entire book on this subject alone!

The only time I buy new storage boxes and baskets is when I need to utilise a specific small space and I don't have anything available. I've got small clear plastic storage boxes for craft items that stack together perfectly on a particular shelf, but I bought them about ten years ago. I have invested in larger, clear storage boxes to stack in the garage for our camping and outdoor items. They are easy to grab for going away and save having to sort through everything each time. They stack into the back of our minibus perfectly and save a lot of time and stress. It is worth investing in storage like this to make life easier, but for compartmentalising smaller items around the house, I try to use what we already have.

CLOCKING OFF

If you're not familiar with the term "clocking off", many factories and similar workplaces had a clock where you'd stick your timecard in upon entering work and it would give it a timestamp. You'd do your work for the day and then "clock off" at the end of the workday, with another timestamp for when you'd finished. It was a way to keep track of who was on time, who was late and who'd be sneaking off on an early dart. It is used mainly now with computer software for capturing when you log in and out to start and finish work. This works well for employees working from home, to prove when you started and finish work.

But as your own boss? Who's watching what time you're working? No one! You are the boss of your own time, so does it matter if you're a few minutes late starting work or finishing a bit early? What's the worst that could happen? You shift unfinished tasks to another time.

Okay, this doesn't sound too bad, and you wanted autonomy over your time, didn't you? Well, it can backfire and what this comes down to is not clocking off when we're supposed to.

When you go out to work, you're *at* work. You're in a completely different environment from home and there are visual cues everywhere to let you know that. Working from home is completely different. The visual cues you have everywhere are that you're at home and this can cause problems when you're trying to focus. Imagine working towards an important deadline, only to be met with a comfy sofa in your line of sight or a pile of washing that's waiting to be put away. It's a little trickier, isn't it?

There's no physical commute from work to home. Whether it's a walk, driving your car or using public transport, the commute journey is a transition that allows our brains and bodies to shift from wearing our work hat to our home hat. You get through the door and kick off your shoes. Maybe someone with a physically demanding job might shower straight away or maybe you'll just get changed into your yoga pants or pyjamas. Whatever happens during this process, it's part of a definitive transition from employee to home-dweller. You don't need to worry about work for the rest of the day, it's a tomorrow problem.

But working from home? It's a lot different. What transition process happens by walking from the kitchen to the lounge that helps you to shift state from home-dweller to business owner? Because those logistical transitions aren't there, it's important we intentionally put them in place for ourselves.

It's important that we have some form of physical or visual cue to "switch off" from work. We've already touched on this in the temporary workstation section. It can be difficult if we haven't got an office door to close, so sometimes, it's something as simple as clearing stuff away or placing a blanket over the office chair to say, "work is done for the day".

When I first started painting at home, I was terrible for nipping out during the TV ad break to do a two-minute paint job on something. There was always something to finish off or fix - and I had a separate work room that I could close the door on! I just couldn't resist nipping in and doing a couple of minutes. It wasn't a healthy balance; I had no discipline. That's also a problem when you love what you do. It's your passion, so why would you want to stop?

Regardless of how much you love your work, you still need to step away. It's too easy to keep going, so putting firm boundaries in place with ourselves is essential.

What I found myself doing last year was remaining seated at my work desk in the evening to do craft work. I was either threading beads, colouring in, or sketching. I had my angle poise lamp to help with the detailed work and convinced myself that I had to sit at the desk to do this. But it was far too easy to slip back into work mode and I'd end up going down a research rabbit hole on the computer or I'd start writing and making notes about work, all because everything was within reach. This is the main reason I bought the small, three-tier trolley to put next to the sofa. Now some of my craft items are there with a small, angled lamp nearby, and I sit on the sofa to do these. It's just a small little tweak to where I store things, but it's had a noticeable impact on me not slipping back into work in the evenings.

To round off this chapter, the tasks you can look at undertaking are:

1. If you don't have a dedicated workspace at home, how can you make the transition to and from a temporary workspace easier and more streamlined? Can you find a dedicated box/bag to use for housing stuff when it's not in use? How can you make it easier to pack stuff away?

2. Have you got any older furniture that could be utilised in a better way? Old bureaus make versatile storage systems, is this something you can do?
3. Can you change your space up to record video and/or audio effectively? Look for folding screens as backdrops or soundproofing, roller blinds, or blank walls, even if it means moving something small out of the way temporarily, like a small side table or picture frame off the wall.
4. Put some visual cues into place for clocking off once you've finished work, particularly if you don't have a separate dedicated office. Sometimes, it's just one simple change that can make a difference.

Chapter 5
Delegation

Do you feel like you're the only one doing things at home? You're knee-deep in managing the entire household but you're also pouring your heart and soul into creating your dream business. Decisions are made over whether to continue keeping the house spotless or whether to scrap any thoughts of cleaning and live in a pigsty whilst you build up enough profit in your business to afford a cleaner.

Time goes on and resentment builds along with the dust. You feel torn between keeping a clean and tidy home and moving your business a step further. It's such a frustrating time. You begin to feel like a failure, procrastinating between home and business, resulting in neither receiving your full attention.

You know there'll come a point where the house slides into chaos and coming back from that is going to be harder to cope with, but you also need to move your business up a level and something has to give. This isn't sustainable and you know changes need to be made.

With different family dynamics in every household, advice on delegating tasks needs to be general, not specific. You might have toddlers around your feet whilst on Zoom calls. You might be surrounded by tired teenagers wandering around the house, auditioning as extras for *Shaun Of The Dead*, not knowing one end of a teaspoon from the other. You might not have kids, but you're struggling to get a partner to share the home responsibilities in an equal way. You might be living on your own and managing everything by yourself. However your household looks, delegation can become difficult.

I used to think that I was proving my worth by doing everything around the house. As a younger adult, I believed it was my role to do the housework and keep things running smoothly. Becoming a single parent at nineteen added to this mindset. I quickly learned that if I didn't do it, it didn't get done.

In recent years, my mindset is working more in my favour. We are at a point where the only washing up I do is on a Friday evening after Am-Dram rehearsal tea breaks. I rarely wash up at home. The teenagers have it under control and I can leave the kitchen safely in their hands once the evening meal is done.

Have I bewitched them? Am I pleading with them and offering insurmountable amounts of pocket money? No, none of that. They just get on with it. They know it's their contribution to running the home as a team.

They do all their own laundry, make packed lunches for school and college and make the evening meal on Tuesday and sometimes Thursday nights. They peel potatoes and carrots when we ask them to and help to make meals when we need an extra hand. They do this without complaining or moaning about how unfair life is. How has this happened?

It's not always been like this, but I am relieved that it's now a steadfast habit for them and us. We don't have room for a dishwasher, so good old Fairy Platinum and Marigolds it is. They don't love it, but they work as a team, create their own rotas between themselves and swap around when needed if one of them is out or working.

GETTING EVERYONE INVOLVED

There are different ways of tackling the problem of getting everyone to pitch in. You know your household best but I'll share what's worked for me and if there's anything you can take from it, then I'll be glad it's helped.

Kids are unlikely to be aware of the full extent of running a home. They only see where and how it affects them. They don't see the mental load (more about that later), they don't see the bills that have to be paid or how tired you are. They can't see that keeping on top of jobs is easier than letting things build up. Their brains aren't grown to capacity. I, for one, would not want to go through puberty ever again!

There are exceptions of course and I do feel we have been lucky in some respects because things could be very different for us. It hasn't always been this way and I've worked hard to get the kids to this point where everyone mucks in.

What we have done is reinforce the essence of teamwork. That we all make the mess, so we should all be responsible for cleaning up. If everyone wants to live in a reasonably nice home, then we need to look after it.

TEAMWORK

Most kids and teens won't have a clue about what to do and when, so create a rota of housework tasks that need to be completed during the week and pin it up where everyone can see it. Do the jobs and tick off when done, maybe put your name by it. At the end of the week, get everyone together and show them the jobs list and what you've done. They may be surprised at the number of jobs on there. They may argue that most of the jobs aren't necessary, but keep at it. Do it again the week after and the week after that. Keep going. Explain that they all need to pitch in. It may take some time, but stand firm. You are not here just to serve everyone else. It's not your role to run yourself into the ground whilst they do nothing.

NATURAL CONSEQUENCES

I've found that natural consequences have worked well for us. The logic is simple:

- If they don't wash their clothes, they won't have any clean ones.
- If they don't wash up, there are no clean dishes for the next meal.

- If you have to clean up because they haven't, you don't have time to give them a lift to a friend's house.
- If you're doing chores that they could be doing, you'll have less energy and so you're too tired to drive them to the Cinema to meet their friends.
- If you're spending time on chores because they haven't done theirs, you're spending less time on your business which affects how much money you make, which means there's no spare money for the Netflix subscription they're nagging for.

If their lack of cooperation starts affecting what they want to do, they'll hopefully start to get the message.

POCKET MONEY FOR YOUNGER KIDS

Draw up a table with a list of jobs down the left-hand column, and across the top row, write the days of the week. For each job, write how much that job is worth. When the kids were a lot younger, we had jobs available for the kids to do for a bit of pocket money. Feeding the cat was 5p, and emptying the dishwasher was 20p. The kids got to choose which jobs they wanted to do and put their initials in the corresponding square on the table when they'd completed the job on a particular day. At the end of the week, I'd reconcile everything, and they'd get various amounts of pocket money.

There were rarely any arguments about this because if they didn't get to do a particular job on one day, there were other days of the week to do it. Patterns emerged for who was comfortable doing what and there were jobs that were varied enough in skill level that they could all do something. Even if it was just getting 30p at the end of the week, the youngest was happy.

Younger kids will need supervising of course, and if they're asked to tidy their rooms, it's highly likely you'll need to be with them, helping. Tidying up isn't an innate skill, they need to learn what goes away first. If your kids aren't tidying their rooms when asked, it's likely down to overwhelm about where to start. Make it a team effort and guide them. One day they'll hopefully just do it without you needing to help and they'll have created the habits needed to keep their space clear and clean.

POCKET MONEY FOR OLDER KIDS

A cash incentive won't work for everyone, but if you feel that it's a fair exchange, then go for it. Make the boundaries super clear though. They need to do the chores properly and without fuss. Don't go letting them get paid for jobs before they've done them, with a promise of "I'll do it tomorrow". This doesn't work and they'll end up in perpetual catch-up mode which doesn't do anyone any favours. They won't be motivated after payday and will likely feel resentful and not do as good a job. Being a teenager is also about testing boundaries, so yes, they're likely to try and bargain with you. It's at this point you have the fate of the next few years in your hands. Give in once and you'll have a five-year battle ahead of you. Stay strong from the start and they'll at least know where they stand, even if they don't like it.

Consider the skills you are helping your kids to build. You're raising them to be healthy, focused, articulate, independent adults. If they can learn these skills now, they'll have no excuse if they move away to university! Try and bring a range of different chores in for them, so they don't feel like they're on the short end of the stick all the time. Mix them up a bit. A bit of cleaning, tidying, washing, cooking, prepping foods and sorting cupboards out. Keep it fresh and hopefully, they'll be willing to learn and feel accomplished.

It's an old cliché that they will thank you for it one day, but it's also true. It just might not be for a while. Maybe about fifteen years.

WHEN IT DOESN'T WORK

It won't work for everyone. If you are raising neurodiverse children, there's a possibility you'll come up against more resistance, or find it much harder to get them to be involved. On the flip side, some may also thrive by having a routine in place. Having worked through all different flavours of parenting over the last thirty years with both my biological children and my stepchildren, I will hold my hand up and say that on several occasions, I got it wrong. I let things slide for an easier life, knowing that it probably wasn't the right thing. It's hard to maintain rules and boundaries when you are completely exhausted and without support from family, CAMHS, or other professionals. Parenthood is a rough ride regardless and if you can get your kids to help with anything at home, then just know that this is a huge win.

SIGNIFICANT OTHERS

It's now 2023 but unfortunately, many households are still living with a gender-based bias regarding who does the housework and who doesn't. It infuriates me and it needs to stop.

The genitals between your legs (however they look and function) *do not* define your ability to get the housework done, or not. Nor do they excuse you from housework because you've been raised to think that it's not your job, or because you've developed some sort of entitlement that's given you an imaginary get-out-of-jail-free card every time the bathroom needs cleaning.

Many of you will be familiar with those two little words "for you", as in "I've done [insert household task of choice] *for you*"... because, of course, every single housework task is your responsibility. And it's been completed on your behalf. For you, you lucky thing.

Call it out! Every time, Call. It. Out.

And if you are the person that says, "for you", please reconsider your language. You do the housework tasks for everyone, including yourself. Not for just one specific person in the home.

Housework tasks are the responsibility of every person in the home who is able to contribute. There will of course be varying degrees of capability due to physical restrictions or executive functioning, but not knowing how to do something, or thinking that it isn't your job isn't a good enough reason. It's been a very long time since schools taught full home economics. The girls were taught how to cook, clean and sew, and the boys were taught how to change spark plugs on engines and make stuff out of metal and wood. I feel strongly that these skills need to make a return to the curriculum, but with a clear update of gender being removed from the equation completely.

So, without home economics at school, kids are learning everything about running a home from us and it's important we raise them with as much equality and inclusion as we possibly can. All capable adults need to know how to do everything it takes to keep their homes running smoothly and be able to explain and show their kids too.

I'm also fully aware that an imbalance in domestic responsibilities may indicate other issues in a relationship. Disclaimer - I am not a relationship professional, therapist or counsellor. I know I need to tread carefully here. I do have lived experience of narcissistic abuse and financial control abuse. I'm sad when I grieve for the time lost to feeling somehow less of a person in previous relationships, but also glad that I can now spot a red flag from twenty paces.

If you feel your partner is deliberately not contributing to housework and running the home, I'm not able to advise you on which way to tackle that. Just know that there is a lot of support online, and particularly on social media, that would be able to help you better than I can. The last thing I would want to do would be to compromise anyone's safety.

THE VILLAGE

I talk a lot about "The Village" - about the phrase "it takes a village to raise a child". Your village is your wider family, your friendship groups, your support network that catches you when you fall, that holds you up when you need it most. In more recent times, I'm hearing a similar analogy - "It takes a village to build a business". So, if you see a lone entrepreneur doing well, know that there's a good chance they've got a business village to help them, whether that's employing a VA, tech support, getting someone to build their website, a social media manager, business coach and/or mentor, staff, etc. That's their village, alongside supportive family and friends. And it's almost impossible to build a successful business without that.

With regards to running your home, if you have grand-parents to help with the kids and have healthy, genuine relationships with them, you are fully blessed. They know exactly how hard it all is and are usually willing to help out when they can, whether that's picking the kids up from school, preparing a meal for you to pop in the oven, doing your ironing whilst you work, mowing the lawn, whatever similar tasks they can take off your hands because they've been there and they know how it goes. They particularly come in handy during school holidays, breaking up the monotony of "I'm bored" plus whatever arguments are being created due to a slow broadband connection. They are absolute diamonds and are to be cherished for as long as they are with you.

But if you don't have family support, you turn to friends as your village. If you decide to run your own business, many friends tend to fall by the wayside. A lot of them "don't get it" unless they also work for themselves. They're unlikely to understand the conflict of working from home and spinning all the plates that come with that. So if support isn't there from family and friends, how do we cope?

CALL THE PROFESSIONALS

Is having a cleaner on your vision board? What about a gardener? All those mundane jobs that you just don't want to do and you'd much rather be working on your business. You've made the decision, it's time to outsource.

I'd highly recommend being strategic about this, however. Don't just employ anyone and think carefully before committing. Think about the jobs you really hate or struggle to do. Those are the ones to outsource first. We have a cleaner, who comes on a weekly basis to clean the kitchen and bathrooms and vacuum the stairs, landings and hallway. We made the decision to get some help after my heart attack left me with much less energy than before. With fibromyalgia also in the mix, there were some days I was finding any physical work impossible. Jobs got put off, and before we knew it, weeks had gone by and the bathrooms would have been a borderline concern with the World Health Organisation. I knew that if I spent my energy on keeping the kitchen and bathrooms clean, then I would have nothing left for anything else for the rest of the week. I'd use up all my energy on cleaning and likely be in bed for the rest of the time.

Outsourcing isn't cheap but then, if you are spending your time cleaning or whatever else you've outsourced, you're not then spending time and energy on the business and not making any money. It's a catch-22 many find themselves in when starting to build a business, and it can sometimes feel like a game of Pontoon for when is the right time to commit to employing someone to lighten your load. It's also got to feel right for you and be affordable and sustainable. It may be that getting a cleaner isn't the first step. If you're fit and healthy, full of energy and happy to clean, then crack on and save yourself that money. But if you just can't manage it, or it just doesn't bring you enough joy or motivation, then it's time.

As business owners, we are encouraged by coaches, mentors and peers to outsource business tasks before we are ready, but for domestic chores, this can seem too much of a stretch. There's a mindset issue because they can't go through your accounts as business expenses! But you have fewer qualms about paying for VA services or anything else that's tax deductible.

Whether you outsource at home is a personal decision. I wasn't sure if I could have someone in my home whilst I was working. I've tried it before and it didn't work out. That's not a problem now we have the right person. We end up having a brew and a chat halfway through. We've become good friends and we're both happy. She's running her business as she wants it and we've got a clean kitchen and bathrooms for the week. It's a good chunk of cash, but we've weighed up the pros and cons and for now, it's worth paying for. Circumstances may change, but for the moment it's peace of mind that those rooms are boxed off for the week.

You're likely outsourcing without realising and there may be some tasks you haven't thought of. Consider what impact outsourcing some of these would have on your circumstances and see if they're worth trying:

- Cleaner,
- Gardener/grounds maintenance/driveway jet wash,
- Window cleaner,
- Wheelie bin cleaner,
- Dog walker/pet sitting services,
- Doggy daycare,
- Childcare - childminder or nursery,
- Breakfast and after-school club/holiday club,
- Online grocery shopping with doorstep delivery,
- Nanny/housekeeper/Au Pair,
- Private chef,
- Meal box subscriptions (think Gusto, Hello Fresh),
- Takeaway/takeaway delivery service/restaurant,
- Taxis/Uber,
- Newspaper delivery,
- Doorstep milk delivery,
- Laundry/ironing services,
- Tailoring services,
- Handyperson services (hanging a shelf, building furniture etc.),

- Chimney sweep,
- Decorating services/furniture painting and upholstery services,
- Clothing subscription boxes (where they've chosen outfits for you),
- Carpet and upholstery cleaning services,
- Professional organiser/decluttering services,
- Outdoor maintenance (gutter and fascia cleaning),
- Rubbish removal/tip runs.

I could probably add a lot more to this list if we went further into everything else that we pay for but this gives you a good starting point.

PERFECTIONISM

The delegator's worst nightmare. This can become a big issue when you need to outsource. I've recognised a trend with business owners in my networks, where perfectionism is rife, and it's holding people back. I know this because I include myself in that number and I am slowly learning to release control as I start to delegate and outsource.

Being satisfied with the standard of housework from kids, teens and partners can sometimes leave you feeling like you'd be as well doing it yourself. They've not done it properly, or at least not to the standard you want. It's a hard lesson to learn, particularly if you thrive on a spotless house but how else are they going to learn?

If you pull them up on it, they're less likely to do it again. Imagine criticising a six-year-old child for not drawing a perfect flower. They wouldn't want to draw a flower again for fear of it being wrong.

Readers of a certain age may remember Harry Enfield's comedy sketch show and his infamous character, Kevin the Teenager.

My favourite sketch was Kevin being asked to wash the car. After staying in bed for most of the day, he finally makes a start but he is disinterested and keeps coming up with lazy, yet ingenious ways to wash the windows, smoking a sneaky cigarette behind the car where his parents couldn't see him. After 24 hours he'd finally finished the task and was rewarded with a crisp five-pound note.

Okay, this is an exaggeration for comedy value, but if teens are that disinterested in the task put in front of them, then what is a layer of criticism going to add? It's harder than it sounds, believe me, I know. I've criticised,

I've got it wrong. I've got so angry at jobs taking too long and making more mess than there was in the first place that I've lost my rag and ended up doing it myself. But all this shows them is that if a job is worth doing, it's only worth doing if it's done perfectly. In business, done is better than perfect. Waiting for perfection results in no action. Failing forward is actively encouraged and this is what to consider when teaching our kids independence.

You're not doing yourself any favours by keeping these tasks to yourself. We need to be freeing up our time, building trust that the kids will eventually learn, and embracing the imperfections in a household that is working together as a team, because that is worth a whole lot more than a perfectly clean home.

To round off this chapter, the tasks you can look at undertaking are:

1. If you've got kids, encourage them to get involved. Reinforce the entire household working as a team.
2. Consider discussing natural consequences if they're not getting the message. Be firm and let this happen. If you continue to give in, you're making a rod for your own back.

3. Consider who your village is. Have you got the right support? Can you reach out and ask for help?
4. Decide whether to outsource some of the housework. What's the job you hate doing the most? Outsource that one first and see what impact it has.
5. Drop the perfectionism. Let the reins go and allow others to help, even if it means it's not done to your standard. The only way to get help is to allow for differences in ability, and the only way they will learn to get better is by doing.

Chapter 6
Decluttering

The dreaded word, clutter. It stirs up all sorts of emotions. It's easy to procrastinate over decluttering because if you've lived with it up to this moment, what's another few days, weeks or months of stepping over things and stuffing clothes into the wardrobe?

It's always a hot topic, with TV series based around tackling it and presenters and teams helping families who are drowning in clutter and chaos. In many of the programmes, their homes have become nothing more than storage boxes for their belongings and they've run out of space to live, so the TV team's intervention is definitely needed. This is a great opportunity for the chosen few, but for the rest of us, we are on our own.

If you feel totally demotivated about decluttering, try writing down ten reasons why you should declutter. What can you see at the end of the process? How does your home look and feel? How will you feel? How will it impact your daily lifestyle? This may help to shift some blocks regarding your emotions around it. Planning time in your diary will also help you to make a start. Knowing that you've allocated half an hour booked here and there to focus on specific areas will make the task feel much more manageable.

DOOM BAGS AND BOXES

I didn't even know these were a recognised thing until I read discussions about them last year. Doom supposedly stands for "didn't organise, only moved", although the word doom also represents the insurmountable junk that's in these boxes and bags. This method is more prevalent within the ADHD community. If your tidying style consists of gathering everything up in the room, dumping it in a bag or box and then leaving it for weeks/months at a time, you have created doom boxes and bags. I used to use this method years ago, by filling a carrier bag full of stuff that needed tidying away. I'd stuff them behind the sofa but then we could never find anything we needed and it used to drive my first husband up the wall.

The only advice I have for these is to allocate half an hour each week to start sorting through them and keep going each week until they're empty. I currently have a large doom box under my desk that's full of paperwork awaiting sorting. I'm not looking forward to it, but I know I need to make a start. If this is something you relate to, at least you're now aware that you're not on your own.

DECLUTTERING – WEIGHT LOSS FOR YOUR HOME

If you are swamped under a tidal wave of clutter, the chances are it's been an accumulation over time. It didn't appear overnight. In that time, things have been put off, ignored and not kept on top of, for whatever reason. It's just what happens and there is no judgement on how and why.

Clutter is like gaining and losing weight. It's never an overnight thing! Changes in lifestyle slip in unnoticed, a bit like possessions coming into the home, but then not doing anything about making space for these new items or keeping on top of the organisation means clutter builds up.

Blitz cleaning and decluttering give us a huge dopamine hit. We get an immediate reward which feels great but how do we keep that momentum going once the initial dopamine hit has worn off?

Why do we expect it to just stay that way? We make promises to ourselves to keep on top of things, but then life happens and clutter gets put to the bottom of the list again. In six-twelve months, we're in the same situation and all that time and energy and effort was for nothing.

KEEPING THE CLUTTER IN CHECK

Think about how long it's all taken to accumulate, then cut yourself some slack about suddenly getting rid of it all. For it to become a sustainable habit, it'll take time to work through and dispose of properly. I'm not talking about responsible recycling or donating to charity when I say this. It's about looking at what space you have, how you use it and whether that item you're holding in your hands really does "spark joy" (Marie Kondo).

Audit/list all your storage places at home – every single drawer, shelf, cupboard, wardrobe, under the beds, in the airing cupboard, the garage, the shed... check everywhere. Allocate each of these to be done throughout the year – whether that's one a day or a few at weekends. Write them down and schedule them in your planner. Keep track of where you're up to. When you're done, start them again in order from the beginning, except this time, hopefully, it'll be much quicker to sort them out. I'd recommend all garage and shed tasks be done over Summer. You don't want to be doing those when it's cold and wet.

By working in this way, you can incorporate keeping on top of the clutter on a daily or weekly basis, without the overwhelm and upset by a mammoth task that will take over your entire weekend - a weekend that you'd most likely want to spend doing something else.

Not every space in your home will need decluttering on a regular basis but by allocating an annual check for each space and integrating this into your annual rota, you ensure that you are only creating space for things you use and not items that haven't seen the light of day for years.

Add in some positive daily habits to putting items away as soon as they are finished with them, or get used to tidying up everywhere with a daily reset, and this should help you keep on top of it. Remember that habits also take time to create. Don't stress about it. Just start with one small space. Declutter with ease and flow.

YOUR CLUTTER THRESHOLD

Where do you draw the line with the clutter? I think this is different for us all and it's simply down to whatever makes us happy at home. Unless there are safeguarding issues, illegal activity, pollution, or animal neglect, it's not our business what anyone else does or how they live if it doesn't affect anyone beyond the front door.

I've been to houses where you've had to climb over a mountain of stuff just to get to the bathroom or clear the floor just to find somewhere to sit, but you were always made welcome.

I've been to a spotless house, where my coffee cup was whisked away from me before I'd finished the last mouthful and it was washed, dried and put away before my brain had time to process what had gone on. I did not feel comfortable there and in turn, not particularly welcome.

Your worth is not defined by your clutter but it could be in the way of inviting new and better things into your life, like new experiences, relationships, and feelings. If you feel that your clutter is a block, then it is a block, and it's time to put a plan together to get it resolved.

THRIFT – THE SABOTEUR IN DISGUISE

We often value our possessions with not just how we feel about them, but also what they're worth in a monetary sense. Conflict arises when you know you just don't use that big fancy food mixer you bought last year with the full intention of wholesome home baking at the weekend, but you just can't bear to part with it because of what it cost. It stays in the cupboard, taking up space, and never getting used. The accessories and tools are impossible to store because they're all shapes and sizes, causing frustration and chaos every time you open the cupboard.

You want to sell it, to recoup as much money as you can. You're already feeling guilty about what that money could have gone towards instead – a much more worthwhile cause. And perhaps you're starting to feel like you're reckless with money if you just give it away. It starts to erode the positive money mindset you've worked so hard to build recently.

Here is your permission to just donate or chuck it. You don't need the money back from it. You don't need to sell it on eBay or Facebook Marketplace. Just donate it. Stick it on a Random Acts of Kindness group on Facebook or your local community page to see if anyone wants it. Someone may be desperate for something like this but lacking the funds to buy one.

Do this and you've done well. You've paid it forward. Your heart will thank you, even if your brain won't. Consider the amount of time, effort and energy spent in disposing of items by selling. You won't get the money back that you paid. It's spent, it's in the past. By investing more of your time into photographing, listing, uploading and dealing with buyers (and timewasters), you may see that it's not worth it for the few quid you'll get from selling the odd item. Consider your own personal hourly rate and whether it's worth your time.

What I don't want to do is have that item cost me even more money by using up my time and energy that I could be investing into writing a new lead magnet for my business or networking, which could lead to potential new clients. My time is better spent doing that than scrabbling around for £20 and £30 here. But, if you are going to sell stuff, maybe do it in one hit, such as at a car boot sale. When you declutter, put your items to one side, in the garage or spare room. When you feel you've got enough to fill the car, pack up and get along to your local car boot. I've come home with hundreds of pounds in my pocket after a day trading at some of our local sales. You may find some dealers at the end of the day are happy to take the rest of the stuff you haven't sold. Whatever you bring home, decide what to do with it. Are you going to save it for another one and add more to it? Or are you going to donate and/or chuck what's left?

By doing it this way, you'll feel the benefit more from selling everything on the day, rather than in dribs and drabs online. You'll be tired, but at least you'll have cleared stuff out of your house, got some fresh air and met some new people. You've sold your second-hand items to others that need them and may not have been able to pay full price for them. Look at it this way and everyone's a winner.

Another thing I've found useful to keep on top of the junk is to have a running bin bag for items that you identify as rubbish as you go about your day-to-day. Anything you spot whilst you're moving around the house that you know needs to go, just grab it and put it in this bag. At the end of the week, tie it up and either put it in the wheelie bin or take it to the tip. I try to keep it somewhere central like on the newel post on the stairs, so I can just pop things in when I'm passing. You'll be surprised at how the bag fills up. This is obviously different from the kitchen and bathroom rubbish that needs emptying on a more frequent basis. I find the kids are great at hoarding stuff like the plastic trays from advent calendars. They tend to make an appearance around March time, along with broken toys or shoes, and other stuff that won't go in the recycling bin.

Try and commit to one large bin bag a week. Or one small carrier bag a day, although the small daily bag method may be better suited to a more active and dedicated decluttering period, rather than a passive one that becomes part of your daily and weekly routine. An intentional combination of both would be even better.

To round off this chapter, the tasks you can look at undertaking are:

1. Write down ten reasons why you should declutter. This will help shift your mindset and motivate you into starting.
2. List all storage compartments in your home. Every drawer, shelf, cupboard, etc. Schedule them evenly throughout the year and commit to decluttering and sorting them, one small space at a time.
3. Work on creating a daily reset routine to keep the house reasonably straight and tidy. It doesn't have to be complicated.
4. Commit to filling one large bin bag a week (or a small bag each day) with clutter to throw.

Chapter 7

Guilty As Charged

Caught between a rock and a hard place wanting to do the best in all aspects of our lives, but then feeling like a failure and unfulfilled? Thinking like this consumes our lives. It feels like we're on a hamster wheel and that we haven't given enough or done enough. We feel that we're lazy for taking a break and that everyone else is coping and we can't. These thoughts spiral into overwhelm and we end up in a depressing whirlwind. If we don't keep our thoughts in check, we become consumed with guilt.

HOUSEWORK GUILT

The constant conflict of do you do the washing or do you write the weekly newsletter that's due out on Friday.

You're faced with these decisions all the time when you work from home. All the housework is in full view wherever you look. Tidying up, laundry, cleaning, washing up, wiping down the sides, clearing the table... It's an endless list.

You're so proud of how much you've achieved so far in your business. You've smashed your work tasks this week. But instead of being proud and celebrating your achievements, you're looking at the state of your home, feeling like a failure because whilst you've been busy working hard for the entrepreneur of the year award, there are no clean clothes for anyone, you've lived off takeaways and oven ready meals all week and the entire family is having a competition of bin Jenga, to see how high they can pile the rubbish before it all falls over. You feel like you're screwed either way and that the only way to business success is to live in a permanent mess.

You know you can only ignore the mess for so long until it tips into chaos and becomes too overwhelming. You find it more and more difficult to concentrate on work because you've realised that your workflow is being affected by your surroundings. You can't work if you're surrounded by chaos. You get to a point where you can't do anything unless you clean up, but then that means losing another day of work.

This wasn't the dream life you were visualising when you decided on being your own boss. There's no ease and flow to your life. You feel you were sold a lie and Bin Jenga was definitely not on your vision board.

Your space doesn't have to be perfect, it just has to be functional. If you look at every room in your home and how it's used, you'll start to identify at what point it needs attention. Can you go a full day without cleaning your kitchen? Probably not. We need clean sides to prepare food and a clean and clear sink to deal with pots and getting the kettle filled, so a quick reset of the kitchen would be to clear the sink – even if this means just stacking the dishes till later - and wiping down the sides.

That's quick, right? And you've got a functioning space to see you through till later on when you've completed your work tasks and you've more time to spend on it.

What about the lounge? Will a quick reset make you feel more comfortable about settling into work? A quick straighten of the sofa cushions, take empty cups to the kitchen, straighten up a few things on the coffee table, any toys or other items off the floor and into a bin or box at the end of the sofa... Would that be enough?

Your bedroom – either make the bed or pull the covers back to air (either providing accomplishment), open the curtains and pick up any clothes off the floor.

These are all straightforward resets for each room. They're not a full clean, but more a visual "cushion plumping" to make things look neat and tidy. This is likely all that's required for you to be able to sit down and start work without getting stressed over the mess. If you've gone through creating a housework rota that we covered in the first chapter and blocked out a specific time to clean and tidy up, then you know that things are under control and you are less likely to become overwhelmed with thinking about housework whilst working.

KEEP YOUR HAT ON

Rule no.1 – You can only wear one hat at a time.

A combination of a well-structured housework rota, a time block system and discipline is key. If you're wearing your work hat, you can't wear your housework hat without swapping. Wearing more than one causes overwhelm and a lack of focus on whichever task you are supposed to be doing.

I used to work in the editorial department of a local newspaper. The deadline to go to press was very early on in the day and a couple of the reporters would wear a hat to let others know that they were working on a hard deadline and were not to be disturbed. Once they had submitted their stories, they removed their hats and took a break. There was no question over whether to interrupt them or not. If the hat was on, you left them alone.

I'm not saying to wear an actual hat around the house, unless you find nothing else is working and you want to give it a go, but find something to make it clear to you, and others around you, that you are in work mode. I use my large headphones for this sometimes, even if I'm not listening to anything. If my cans are on, the kids know not to disturb me. Perhaps an elastic bracelet or something would be enough for you to distinguish between work mode and home mode, or changing your shoes. Maybe have specific playlists for different tasks. There are lots of things you could try. Something that serves to remind you that you've set your intention to work on your business, or to do something else.

Having some form of work uniform will also help. Consider the dress code that you may have integrated into your employment contract for yourself from the efficiency chapter.

SCHOOL HOLIDAYS

The six-week summer break is an outdated model. Originally put in place because kids weren't attending school anyway at that time of year due to helping with harvesting on the farms, the schools decided to close the doors and open again in September. Kids don't work like that anymore, so having this six-week block each year when we're expected to put on a clown nose and entertain the kids is a nightmare that most parents dread.

If you don't have help from grandparents or other family members to help with school holidays, it can become difficult, almost impossible at times, to work on your business during school holidays. The easiest way of tackling it is to not fight it. If you're able to stop work for a few weeks, then do so. You can still schedule your social media content to maintain some continuity there.

Work it into your business strategy when you look at the year ahead. I've also found that most people, whether they have kids or not, anticipate changes in work patterns over the summer. A lot of people are on holiday, it feels too hot to be bothered some days and a large portion of home-based business owners work this way to be flexible with their family commitments.

I'm okay with the six-week holidays now I've reframed them and the kids are getting older. There are no school runs, packed lunches or school uniforms to deal with. The weather is usually great and we just switch on feral mode for six weeks. I've not always felt like this about it but until they're all adults and doing their own thing, there's not much I can do.

As the kids get older, it's obviously easier to explain to them why you still need to work. They have a better understanding of money and paying bills. Younger kids are going to have a harder time with this. It can become stressful for everyone. I can't emphasise enough to plan out the six-week break well in advance, don't just let it happen. We've broken it up in previous years with having some time away in weeks three and five, which means there's just the two-week stretch in the middle. The rest is broken up with time away, or at least one day out a week to visit somewhere different.

PROCRASTINATION

The definition sourced from dictionary.com:

> ***"The act or habit of procrastinating, or putting off or delaying, especially something requiring immediate attention."***

Procrastination is a sneaky so-and-so. It's that sneaky, you may not realise when you are procrastinating. It comes in many different guises:

- ***Procrasti-cleaning*** – when you suddenly develop the urge to empty the cupboard under the sink and scrub it to within an inch of its life. To declutter, buy clear storage boxes, organise everything with vinyl cut labels and admire your work that's taken the last five hours. You do this all because you've convinced yourself it's taken priority over writing the copy for your new website.
- ***Procraftinating*** – You know that creativity is good for your soul, so rather than do work that'll move your business forward, you convince yourself you need an hour out of your day to craft. Cue hyper-focus mode on your craft of choice and you lose the entire day to your project, becoming an expert in the process. You've forgotten to eat or stay hydrated, you've barely moved from your seat so your back and legs have seized, you need to pee like there's no tomorrow and now you're panicking because the blog you should have written today which is due tomorrow, simply hasn't been done.

- ***Procrasti-faffing*** – Mooching around the house with general malaise, trying to muster up the right vibe to start the priority project with a looming deadline. You end up faffing with stuff, plumping cushions, lining books up on the shelf and swapping ornaments around on the sideboard to see if it looks better than before. What you're really doing is looking for a dopamine hit with a noticeable difference to your living environment, whilst avoiding that big tech job you know needs your attention. You simply don't have the motivation to do it, so you keep yourself busy, convincing yourself that you'll start it in five minutes. Another day has gone and you're no further on. Oh, and your sideboard display doesn't look right now, so you move everything back to how it was. Moving that photo frame was *not* the answer. You have achieved absolutely nothing today.

The point I'm making is that we are all guilty of procrastination. It's a form of self-sabotage. We feel we're just not in the right mindset for something, or we're not feeling energetically aligned to do a particular piece of work. We can give ourselves a hundred and one reasons to procrastinate but the bottom line is, we just aren't motivated enough to get the work done, and that's something we need to combat in order to stop feeling guilty about wasting our own time.

There are lots of ways you can break procrastination:

- Change your state. Get up out of your chair and move to a different room in your home,
- Use the five-second rule method suggested by Mel Robbins. Every time you need to do a task, countdown from five to zero then get up and do it. No bartering with yourself, no promises. Just do it straightaway,
- Use a personal mantra for the times when you're feeling a bit stuck. This could be based on your main goals. Remind yourself of your goals and ask yourself if what you're doing right now is bringing you closer to those goals or carrying you further away. Take the appropriate action,
- Revisit your goals and check to see that they are motivating enough for you. If not, then maybe it's time to find some different goals or break them down into milestone mini-goals. You'll be more inclined to do the work if you can see the next milestone is near.

Sometimes procrastination is exhaustion in disguise. Obviously, if you're tired, take a break. Don't work through or give yourself a hard time. I've beat myself up time and time again for just not getting my act together. I thought the lethargy I was feeling was a lack of motivation and drive. It turned out to be a bad case of anaemia and I needed iron tablets to restore my energy and strength. When I start procrastinating now, I stop and think about the reasons why. It's about digging deep and picking apart why you're avoiding important tasks. You may surprise yourself with the answers.

Without going too much into the psychology of all of this (because I am not qualified to do so), sometimes we just need to give ourselves a good old kick up the backside. Mindset coaches can help with problems like this if they are prolonged issues. Do your due diligence, read testimonials and find one through a personal referral. Being self-motivated is a huge undertaking and there is nothing wrong with asking for help. We will all need it at some point.

THE MENTAL LOAD

The mental load is a recognised phenomenon carried mostly, although not exclusively, by mums - the mother, the caregiver, the one that generally makes everything happen at home, the one who sees all the jobs that need to be done where others fail to recognise them, the one that sees the sticky handprints on the bannister rail where others are oblivious - the one that knows to order toothpaste *before* the whole tube runs out.

There's more to running a home and raising kids than just the mechanics of doing the housework and keeping everyone fed and watered. If it were that simple, there'd be no issues – we'd just create a check-list every day, tick everything off and wow, our job is done. No emotion, just working on the tasks at hand.

As great as it sounds, that's not how it works. It's the difference between parenting and babysitting. The babysitter will just focus on the kids for the time they are paid for and nothing else. They don't need to plan anything in advance, just entertain the kids for a few hours and make sure they're fed, watered and kept safe.

Imagine doing this every single day of your life but as well as being responsible for feeding, watering and keeping them safe, you're also wondering:

"What do I make for tea tonight? Do I need to take something out of the freezer? If I have the chicken tonight, does that mean I'll need to go

shopping again before the weekend? Did I even order the grocery shop? I'm sure we're low on toothpaste. Who's left the hand towel on the floor again? That reminds me there's a small leak on the tap that needs looking at. Can I do that myself? Will the plumber come out for such a small job? How much is it going to cost for a call-out? Can we afford it? I'll have to use the money saved for school shoes. I'm sure there's a parents' evening coming up soon. If I get a wash done today, will I get a chance to hang it outside or will it have to go on the airer and take up space over the weekend? The weather forecast says 20% chance of rain, but I can't decide. What if it rains whilst I'm out and the washing gets soaked? Why are there no towels left in the airing cupboard? I've just remembered the youngest is at a birthday party tomorrow and I've forgotten to buy a gift and card. Will people judge me for putting some cash in the card? Will they be expecting a perfectly wrapped gift? What will the other parents think of me? Did the PTFA ask for chocolates or bottles for the raffle for the fair? How long have those leftovers been in the fridge? Shall I chance it or throw out yet more food? Have I even got time to make tea in-between football practice and scouts? It is the church parade this

weekend, right? Or is it next? Is there a reason why the eldest walked out of school on their own this afternoon? Have they fallen out with their friends? Are they being bullied? Are my children happy? Am I a good enough parent? What am I missing? Should I be doing more?"

And breathe.

That's what the mental load looks, feels and sounds like. And it never ends. It's often carried by the person in the home that makes Christmas and birthdays "happen". The one that thinks about things well in advance, promising themselves they'll be better organised next time, getting themselves stressed because everything is last minute again, undertaking everything with the best of intentions and always feeling like things would have been perfect had they just done this or just done that. It's a curse and I'm not sure it's one that will ever be fully resolved. As carers, we tend to carry this mental load with us regardless and it's exhausting.

The only way to lighten the load is to prioritise your mental, physical and emotional health and well-being. Put yourself first, emotionally regulate and forgive yourself for not having the capacity to "do it all".

Because no one on this earth can do it all.

To round off this chapter, the tasks to consider undertaking are:

1. Identify some form of physical or visual reminders for when you are in work mode, and when you are in home mode.
2. Plan out the school holidays in advance. Decide whether you're going to be working or not. Make sure you've got an ideas bank of days out, things to do and general stuff to keep the kids occupied, as well as yourself.
3. Identify what you turn to when you procrastinate. Do some work around what kind of tasks you avoid, and why you avoid them.
4. Breathe. Give yourself as much forgiveness and compassion as possible. You are not everything to everyone else. You are not superhuman, there is no such thing.

Chapter 8

Self-Care

If I asked you to be honest about your self-care strategy, what would you say? Would you tell me that you take care of yourself first and foremost? That it's a priority in your life? Would you tell me that it's an essential part of your routine and you put it above and beyond everything else going on in your life?

Or would you tell me you don't even know what self-care is anymore? You dress it up as a trip to the supermarket on your own without the kids or having a bath in peace once they've gone to bed. Or do you see self-care as just spa days, nail treatments, detox retreats and pamper sessions so you think that you can't do self-care because you haven't got time or funds available?

There's nothing wrong with all of those and they can form part of a wider strategy, but that isn't what true self-care is about.

TRUE SELF-CARE

The self-care spectrum is much bigger than that and encompasses every part of our staying healthy, whether physically, emotionally or mentally. It is every single part of us taking care of ourselves and it covers so much more than mud face masks and luxury bubble baths, spa days and champagne.

Self-care will also look different to everyone, although aspects will be similar. My take on self-care is this:

To undertake an action in any aspect of my life that my future self will thank me for.

How simple does that sound? I focus on what future Nic will thank me for. And since changing that way of thinking, I take better care of myself.

My simple self-care strategy includes:

- Staying hydrated by drinking lots of fluids throughout the day so I don't get headaches and dehydration. My skin looks better and my body works better with the fluid it needs,

- Eating a healthy meal to give my body the nutrients it needs to function properly,
- Saying no to unhealthy foods to give my body a break from dealing with additional stresses such as weight gain, detoxing and cardiac disease,
- Moving my body so it works properly,
- Taking my herbs and supplements every day to aid recovery and function,
- Walking outside to get fresh air into my lungs and oxygen to my brain,
- Showering in the evening so I'm not rushing in a morning,
- Sticking to my morning routine to make sure I'm motivated for the day,
- Sticking to my evening routine to make sure I sleep better so I'm not as tired in the morning,
- Creating a business strategy I can stick to, to ensure I build a business that will support us financially as we get older,
- Being kind to myself when I'm having a hard day as life is difficult at the best of times,
- Carving out time just for me to focus on myself so I can feel energised and refreshed,
- Taking a break when I feel tired because I don't want to push my body further and possibly into a fibro flare,

- Removing toxic people from my life so I can thrive and be happy,
- Setting boundaries with others so I can protect my time and energy,
- Setting boundaries with myself because I know I need to in order not to overdo things.

They're not complicated things to do, but they do get overlooked as they're not sold as self-care. What better way of caring for yourself than giving your body what it needs?

Identify what you do for self-care. List ten things you can improve upon to take better care of yourself. When you plan out your week (covered in the time block section), block out your self-care time first and foremost. Analogies about putting your own oxygen mask on first, or not being able to pour from an empty cup are bang on.

BURNOUT

There's no badge of honour for burnout. It's not an achievement or goal you would ever wish to reach. Believe me when I say that burnout is a horrible place. It does feel like Hell some days and not a day goes by where I don't regret having pushed myself too far.

One of the biggest problems with burnout is that you simply don't know your limits until you've surpassed them. And the journey back from burnout is a lot more complicated than the journey that took you there in the first place.

I've worked through a lot of shame around hitting burnout. I felt I should have seen it coming and changed track accordingly, that I should have known better. There is a lot I could have done to stop this from happening - hindsight is wonderful, yes? But when you're in flow, feeling like you're working *in the moment*, you feel like you're smashing through your task list and want to keep going. You always think you'll be okay, what's the worst that will happen? You'll be tired tomorrow, so what? You can rest, right? You can always rest tomorrow.

Hold that thought.

OVERWHELM CREEP

Have you heard of the frog in hot water analogy? If you put a frog into hot water, it'll jump straight out. The frog knows the hot water will kill it so takes the appropriate action. If you put a frog into cold water and slowly heat that water, the frog won't move. It'll stay there, unaware of the change in temperature until it's too late. The water finally reaches temperature. The frog dies. The environment in which the frog has found itself has changed incrementally, almost unnoticeable, with no severe changes apparent. Sound familiar?

Sometimes we don't know we are in over our heads until it's too late. It may not be the big curve balls that knock you for six. It could be all the smaller changes to your lifestyle that happen over a period of time, until one day, you realise you've been treading water that long it's become second nature and a permanent feature in your day-to-day routine. Then just the smallest thing could tip you over the edge - the straw that breaks the camel's back.

This is what happened to me.

MY BURNOUT STORY

I was diagnosed with fibromyalgia in December 2018. Determined not to be beaten, I kept going and pushed through the daily pain and discomfort. It was vital I stayed mobile and my doctor supported this.

In January 2020, we'd just moved for the second time in twelve months, to where we are now. The rented farmhouse was only ever going to be a temporary stay which we knew when we moved there the February before.

I'm involved in a local Amateur Dramatics group and Panto week was hectic. The Aladdin production was chaos behind the scenes. Props needed finishing; costumes had been missed. I picked up doing a lot of the work, including making a ridiculous Widow Twankey laundry dress from scratch a few hours before the first performance. I got caught up in the momentum of the week, throwing myself into finishing jobs and ignoring my own work. Some people weren't pulling their weight and animosity grew. I ended up powering through the week to get things finished and boxed off.

I was coping well but knew at the back of my mind I was running on adrenaline and it wouldn't last. I just needed to get through production week, then I could take a break. We got through it and I started to make plans for an easier following week.

But I'd forgotten on the Monday that I had a dental appointment in the morning and in the afternoon the gas safety check was being done at home. By this time, I was exhausted, and aching to sleep but I had the school run to do as well and I was starting to weep like a child who'd run themselves tired into an emotional mess. I just kept thinking, I can rest soon, just another day or so and I can take some proper time out.

The next day I was up and ready for a business workshop in the city centre. I'd booked it a couple of weeks prior, as I hadn't expected to be as busy as I was, and this was to be an enjoyable day just for me. I met some amazing people and it was the first day I shared with others my ideas for building the Platespinning Academy which I received great feedback for.

It was an enjoyable day with a great buzz. Although I felt tired, my brain was starting to re-energise with all the new ideas. I'd started to feel really tired around the half-three mark but just put it down to being out for the day. When I got back, Ade was making tea, so I got a brew and sat down on the sofa.

And that's when things started to change.

I started to feel tired. Extraordinarily tired. I could barely speak and ended up sleeping through teatime. I woke about half past seven. Ade brought me some pasta bolognese he'd put to one side for me. I ate it on the sofa, propped up on cushions. I could barely find the strength or coordination to use the cutlery.

I'd not felt this tired in a long time. I went to bed but couldn't sleep. My forehead was boiling. I usually use heat pads when I have a headache or migraine, but this was different. I used a cold flannel and took paracetamol to try and reduce my temperature. It wasn't like a normal headache, it was across my forehead and it was a very strange sensation. I felt hot in general but this going on with my head concerned me more. I fell asleep eventually, but it took a while, wedging the cold flannel across my head, trying to get comfy.

I woke up around half past three with pain in my back. I thought I must have fallen asleep in a strange position, so I started to move, which usually helps relieve it.

It did not relieve the pain.

I sat up in bed and tried to stretch it out. It didn't work. In fact, the pain got worse. It was like someone had drawn a line across my back, from the outside of one shoulder blade to the other.

I woke Ade up and told him I didn't feel well. I wasn't sure what was happening, but I didn't like it. It's easy with fibro to dismiss any aches/pains/nausea/feeling ill for fibro symptoms, and it was a fine line as to whether I should just try and go back to sleep, but my gut was telling me this wasn't fibro.

By now, I was lying back and scared to move. I didn't know what to do. After a telephone triage with 111, an ambulance arrived. The crew did some very quick blood prick tests, as well as an ECG. Everything came up okay, and I had started to feel a little better but was still unsure of whether that was down to relief that the paramedics were with me. They decided to take me to the hospital anyway, as there was an extra test they could do there.

My experience in the emergency department was horrendous. Following numerous blood tests and being made to walk to the x-ray department even though I'd already smashed my knee after collapsing in the corridor, I was left to sit on a plastic chair in another busy corridor whilst the results came back. A few hours later, I was finally admitted after my blood tests indicated I'd had a minor heart attack. I'm grateful to say the care changed drastically for the better once the in-patient band was put on my wrist.

So, I did finally get my rest! Just not as expected – in a hospital bed for six days. I made the most of it and slept when I could. I switched off to everything that was going on in the outside world because it had become blindingly clear that I now had to make myself the priority above everything and everyone else. This was a very different attitude I needed to take. I wasn't used to it, but I knew that if I didn't switch off to external stressors, I'd be making things a lot worse. I was mortified that I'd found myself in a cardiac ward at the age of forty-five. I was the youngest patient until my last night there and I am still, to this day, processing what happened.

I was transferred to another hospital the following Monday for an angiogram before finally being discharged. They caught a nerve doing the procedure and I was back at the hospital four days later in the worst pain I've experienced.

My brain checked out for a few months. I couldn't concentrate on anything like reading or knitting. I struggled with conversations. I could watch TV but nothing that required focus and attention. I slept. A lot. The one and only job I had to focus on for the next few weeks was rest and recuperation.

I had to take powerful blood thinners for the following year and I'm now on aspirin for life. As a result of taking aspirin, I also take medication daily to protect my stomach. This can affect the absorption of vital vitamins and minerals from my food. As a result, I get anaemia frequently, causing plummeting energy levels and less oxygen to my brain, which causes brain fog. I take iron supplements when my levels dip, which causes constipation, so I end up in more pain and discomfort. The cycle continues.

All these health issues are because of one medication. Because I had a heart attack. Because I hit burnout.

Despite the above, I also consider myself lucky, because another alternative could have been that I wouldn't be here.

BOUNDARIES WITH YOURSELF

If you know you are terrible with boundaries, it's imperative that you work hard to put them into place, starting with yourself. It may not sound important, but they are easy to forget about when we've pushed ourselves too far. This is more of a problem when we are working on projects that we absolutely love and don't have a natural off switch.

There's nothing wrong with using alarms, post-its, visual prompts and self-imposed rules to keep us safe and on track. If that's what we need to do to maintain a healthy balance, then so be it. The next hurdle is ensuring that we make a conscious effort to commit to our boundaries.

If you think back to the stories that I've shared with you about always wanting to keep myself busy, being a perfectionist, struggling to delegate and the stress life has put on us with raising bereaved children and dealing with the fallout of that, it's no wonder I ended up in hospital.

I know so much more now about looking after myself but I can't turn back the clock. What I can do is make sure I'm saying no to things that don't concern me or aren't important or relevant, making space in my days and weeks to take time out and breathe. I'm not prepared to test my limits again. I get early warning signs and it's taking notice of those and acting on them that keeps me on the right side of overwhelm.

I've had my scare. I don't ever want you to go through the same.

To round off this chapter, the tasks to consider undertaking are:

1. Write down ten things you can identify that are self-care for yourself.
2. Do these need to be integrated as habits? Check back to the habits chapter for ways to make this happen.
3. Create a self-care strategy for yourself. Is there a prompt you can use in your planner or diary

to tick off when you've completed self-care tasks for yourself?

4. Start putting some boundaries into place. Learn to say no. If you've been a yes person for years, this is going to be more difficult but you owe it to yourself to put yourself first, always.

Chapter 9
Curveballs

Curveballs – those problems that life throws in every now and again to see how you cope, the severity of which is a highly subjective matter. I see the word curveball used in varying contexts. Some use the term to explain missing their train, or the car breaking down. I'm not talking about those; I see those as daily life hiccups.

I'm talking about the big ball ones. The ones you don't want to think about or ever deal with.

The problem is, you don't always get a warning of when they will strike. Life can change in an instant. We are all only ever one phone call away from our lives changing forever. It's not pleasant to think about but loss and change are inevitable parts of our journey through life.

Living through challenging times is so hard. With any change to our status quo - regardless of whether it's thrust upon us or something we choose - we need a period of adjustment to find our feet with our new normal.

Think about big life changes that may be planned or expected – a new baby, a new job, moving house. However welcome these may be, they still upset daily routines and structures. But, we have time to prepare, to organise, to brace ourselves for the change.

Other changes can hit us like a tidal wave with no warning – bereavement, relationship breakdown, an accident or serious illness. It's not nice to think about these, but if our lives aren't following some sort of routine or structure already, then how do we even begin to cope when the big curveballs hit? Do you have emergency plans in place for if or when the worst happens?

I'm asking you now to step out of your comfort zone and think about what you would do if something big happened tomorrow that would throw your world into chaos. What are your instincts telling you to do? What are your priorities?

Whilst it may be reasonable to suggest that you'd know what to do, extreme emotion does strange things to our rational thoughts when we are in the moment. We may not be in a place mentally or emotionally where we can think straight and instead go into a state of fight, flight, or freeze. Whatever is going on, we are not our rational thinking selves and so perhaps an emergency plan is something to consider and plan for in advance, in the hope that it's not needed.

As a family, we've been in the thick of some meteor-sized curveballs over the last few years and I believe that exaggeration is well deserved. Our lives have changed beyond recognition; we were simply not prepared for the days, weeks, months and years that lay ahead. We had to adapt quickly, going from a household of three to a household of eight overnight when my stepchildren lost their mum. This impacted all parts of our lives. The shopping bill increased fourfold, mealtimes became manic, the laundry became an impossible task. Stuff was piled everywhere and we had to quickly create permanent bedrooms instead of just weekend ones. Extra furniture for storage became a priority instead of having everything in bags and boxes. We were plunged into complete chaos, barely having time to stop and think. But the world didn't stop for us to catch our breath. The pause button we desperately needed didn't exist.

FIREFIGHTING MODE

When life gets turned upside down, our default state often turns to firefighting mode. Meeting the needs of the moment as they happen in real-time, rather than putting plans into place that will be helpful tomorrow and for the longer-term future. When everything becomes the priority all at once, life feels impossible. Stress levels are raised and there's no room to breathe.

Adrenaline kicks in and our heightened anxiety state has us on high alert, enabling us to deal with the insurmountable problem pile that throws issues at you faster than an Aldi checkout operative. What would normally be a small task or minor inconvenience suddenly grows horns and becomes catastrophic. In tackling them, they consume all our energy and thoughts.

This fight-or-flight response was how our prehistoric ancestors survived out in the wild. It enabled them to fight the bear or to run away from it. But modern-day living doesn't need to fight bears to survive and turning down a nervous system that's at Defcon One can be difficult - it won't happen with the click of a finger. This response is helpful in times of crisis, such as a car accident or the need to drive to the hospital in a quick but careful manner to respond to an emergency. It helps us to perform CPR when someone has gone into cardiac arrest. It helps us to flee a burning building. It helps us make better decisions in the moment with a sharpened brain, assuming we don't freeze with fear.

But living in this state on a long-term basis is where it becomes an issue. We were never meant to live in a permanent state of anxiety. Modern-day life has brought with it an epidemic of stress-related health issues just with living a so-called normal life. Throw big curveballs into the mix and we are left in a permanent state of overwhelm, and it's just not sustainable. We need a plan, a map, something to work with. We need some kind of instruction manual to do the thinking for us when we can't.

SURVIVAL INSTINCTS

As humans, the things we need to survive are relatively simple. *Maslow's theory of motivation* highlights our needs at different levels based on our motivation to achieve them, creating a hierarchy of needs. At the most basic level are our physiological needs of water, food, warmth and shelter.

Imagine you end up stranded on a deserted island, with no one else to help. What do you do first? My first keynote talk as a professional speaker uses the film *Castaway* as an example of this. Tom Hanks (or Chuck as his character in the film) finds himself alone, washed up on a deserted island after a plane crash. No one else survives, he's on his own.

The first thing he does is try and build a shelter from the wind and rain. He finds coconuts to eat and drinks rainwater that collects on leaves. He's motivated to do these because he needs them to survive.

Once his most basic needs are met, he starts to build and improve his surroundings as time goes on. He's motivated to find a better shelter and to make a fire to stay warm and cook crab.

Once our physiological needs are met, we then look at safety. In our modern-day world, this could look like making sure mortgage or rent payments are met so we can stay in our homes. The hierarchy goes further - we improve our surroundings, we harvest and maintain relationships, working on aspects of our lives to improve, to get to the next level of needs.

We could be anywhere within this hierarchy, just doing our thing and minding our own business, but throw a meteor-sized curveball into the mix and we return to our most basic of needs first. This is where our priorities lie. From this, we can start to form our own survival plan.

To read further on our motivational needs, Google *Maslow's hierarchy*.

BASIC NEEDS DURING A CRISIS

Some of these may sound extreme but this is only designed as a temporary measure. Don't take on any more emotional burdens regarding feeling guilt or shame about shortcuts for the moment. You are giving yourself an amnesty from normal life functioning because that's what is required right now. This is just one part of creating compassion for yourself.

FOOD AND NOURISHMENT

- Online shopping – get someone else to put this together for you if you are unable to right now or have someone get it for you from the shop.
- Buy ready meals or simple meals that don't need much thought. Open and serve, minimal prep foods. Make sure you are getting plenty of fruit and veg. Use pre-cut - whatever removes any or all of the prep stages.
- Use disposable paper plates/bowls/cups/plastic cutlery if suitable. Do

not feel guilty about this. It's a temporary change to give you a bit of headspace back.

- Amazon Prime – for everything else you need to buy. Get someone else to order for you if you can't. If you don't already have it, it's (currently) £8.99 per month and you get next-day delivery on most items - some can even arrive the same day.
- Takeaway, local bakery, a deli for cooked foods (if budget allows). Use delivery services where you can.
- Plenty of fluids, keep hydrated. When you are out of a normal routine it's easy to forget to drink.
- Get some extra milk to keep in the freezer in case you run out. Take it out before bedtime and leave it in the sink overnight. Give it a good shake in the morning and wipe down the condensation on the outside before putting it in the fridge.
- Bread – keep a couple of spare loaves in the freezer for emergencies but try and use them within four weeks. You can always swap them over with fresher loaves.
- If you feel able to cook a meal, try and double up the amount so you've another meal ready just to reheat without needing to cook.

HOUSEWORK / MAINTAINING A FUNCTIONAL SPACE

- Keep the kitchen sink as clear as possible.
- Keep the kitchen sides as clear as possible and wiped down, or even just one for food prep.
- If washing up is piling up (and there's no dishwasher), stack plates in a bin liner or carrier bag and leave until you are ready.
- Kitchen roll for wiping everything down – it's quicker than dishcloths and just throw it away when done.
- Bathroom – don't even bother. As long as the floor is dry and the toilet is clean, everything else can wait.
- Washing – priorities are socks/underwear, school uniforms, t-shirts and tea towels. Everything else can wait.

FIRE SAFETY

- Before bedtime, check the cooker and hob are off. Switch small appliances off at the wall.
- Keep oven gloves away from the cooker, even when you're not cooking.

- Check all rooms before bed and switch any electrical items that aren't required off at the wall socket.
- Close all internal doors at night – the most important one is the kitchen door. Encourage the kids to close their bedroom doors if they usually keep them open.
- Keep your key by the front door so you know where to find it in the dark quickly, on a hook out of sight from the outside.
- Check your smoke detectors are working.
- Talk through a simple fire safety plan with your family. Printouts are available online via local Fire Services. Most primary schools have visits from the Fire Service in Key Stage one and two, so they may already know the drill, but it's still worth going through it with them.

These are just some basic points on getting started with an emergency plan. I suggest creating something like this before you need it. The last thing you want is to be thinking about things like this whilst going through a crisis.

Take the thinking out of the equation. Trust in yourself that you have made the best judgement call beforehand by creating your plan.

If we'd had something like this put together before our big curveball in 2014, we'd have coped so much better and the financial, physical and mental impact may have been much less severe. But of course, you don't know what you don't know. You never think the worst is going to happen. I never thought we'd find ourselves in such a severe situation. It's something that happens to other people. That's what I thought, anyway.

To round off this chapter, the task to consider undertaking is to put together an emergency plan for your household. What's your crisis plan? How are you going to keep things going? It's a hard question to answer but try and put something down, even if it's just a bullet-pointed list with some small actionable steps.

Chapter 10
Food

This isn't a comprehensive section. There is so much to consider for food, that I simply cannot cover it all here. It's enough for an entire book just by itself - which will be a future project - but I've given an overview to get things started and on the right track.

OUR FUEL

Food is our fuel. It's the stuff that keeps our bodies running and working for us. It's one of the biggest parts of our lives and we can't manage without it. It's capable of evoking a range of emotions and problems. Food can soothe and comfort. What it can also be is a source of stress, with allergies, intolerances, textures, over-cooking, undercooking, food poisoning, use-by dates, packaging and unnecessary additional ingredients like flavour enhancers and colourings.

We need to eat every day and regularly. Not eating at all causes problems with blood sugar levels and not eating balanced meals causes health issues over time. It sounds like a nightmare, doesn't it?

It's also a source of stress when you're trying to think of what to make for dinner in the evenings, every single day of your life! It can become draining to keep coming up with ideas, only for the picky eaters at the table to make you wonder why you bothered in the first place! It's so easy to just shove fish fingers and chips in front of the kids each night. No arguments, no stress, just shove everything in the oven and it's done.

It's okay occasionally, but for a balanced diet, we need a wider range of foods. I'm not a qualified nutritionist or health professional, so if you need additional support for your diet, please find someone who is qualified to do so. Any foods I discuss in this section are coming from my common sense of what I believe to be an okay diet for a busy family. It's not perfect, but it's okay.

MEAL MANAGEMENT

Getting a meal on the table each night sounds straight-forward - surely there's not much to think about. It'd be great to have a magic wand that conjured up a healthy, balanced, well-presented meal for everyone each night. I wish!

But there's so much more to consider for that one meal in an evening:

- When was the last time you ate this meal?
- Are your meals varied enough?
- Are there dietary requirements to consider?
- Will the kids even eat it?
- Do you have all the ingredients available?
- If there's anything to take out of the freezer, have you done it?
- Is it defrosted? Can you cook it from frozen?
- How long does it take to cook?
- How complicated is the recipe?
- Are the portion sizes correct?
- Can you have everything hot at the same time?
- Will it be cooked enough?
- What if someone gets food poisoning?
- What if you burn it?

- How much is it costing?
- Have you got time to make it?
- Is there any prep to do beforehand?
- Have you even got the energy to make it?

That entire list looks exhausting, and that's without buying the food to cook.

THE GROCERY SHOP

Before we can cook it, we need to buy it. If you're not already using an online grocery service, I would lovingly ask you to give it consideration, to give you back some time and energy. Delivery slots are available for as little as a pound (mostly a Wednesday or Thursday teatime). You'd likely spend more on that in fuel to get there and back.

If you absolutely love going to the supermarket, maybe the next bit isn't for you, but it does highlight just how much time and energy you're spending on it, and if these are aspects of your life you are looking to stream-line (you bought this book, so I'll assume the answer is yes), give some consideration of what a visit consists of. A walk-through of going to the supermarket looks something like this:

- Make sure the shopping bags are in the car (first hurdle),
- Drive to the supermarket,
- Find somewhere to park,
- Find a trolley that doesn't have wonky wheels,
- Check your shopping list (assuming you've made one, or remembered to bring it),
- Go around the store looking for all the items you need,
- Pray they haven't changed the layout since your last visit,
- Get to the checkout, take everything out and put it onto the conveyor belt,
- Let the cashier scan everything and put it all back into the trolley. You might try and pack the bags at this point unless it's Aldi or Lidl,
- Realise that the groceries take up twice the amount of space repacking the trolley like this, and there's not enough space,
- Get back to the car, avoiding other vehicles and pedestrians with a loaded trolley that won't push in the direction you want it to,
- Pack the bags into the boot whilst stopping the trolley from rolling away into someone else's car,
- Take the trolley back to the trolley station,

- Drive home,
- Bring all the heavy bags into the kitchen in as few trips as possible,
- Unpack and put everything away,
- Realise you've just spent two hours on something that could have been resolved with the click of a button.

And breathe!

Okay, if you're shopping at Aldi or Lidl, you have no choice but to go to the shop. I love both of these supermarkets so I visit them as part of my bulk-buying shopping trips, but if you're at one of the larger supermarkets, then why wouldn't you be ordering online? For a small amount of delivery charge, you can have someone else pick your items for you and have them delivered directly to your door, taking out all that time and energy spent doing it yourself.

ONLINE GROCERY ACCOUNTS

Prior to 2014, I did try online grocery shopping but felt that just getting the online account sorted and then trying to find everything I wanted was too much hassle. Clearly my motivation for learning to do it better changed when our needs changed to feed a household of eight and not three. If you've tried it and found it hard work, give it another go. You can order annual delivery passes which make it even cheaper, and I've found that by having the delivery pass, I can split our shopping into two orders a week with no extra costs. This makes it more flexible for us, particularly in summer when the fruit and veg will go off quicker. We can just buy for the next few days.

You can set up a standard weekly shopping list and use that as your starting point, then just add in other items that you need, but don't always need to buy each week. I've found a way to keep on top of my dynamic shopping list each week is to have a post-it note on each week-to-view spread of my diary/planner. On this I write anything that is getting low or runs out, so we can order it on the next shop.

Another thing I do is look at the next week ahead and check my menu plan for any ingredients we may need that we have run out of. They go on the post-it note for the week before and I make sure it's ordered in advance.

This also works well for birthdays, when we might need to buy a cake, or some chocolates or sweets. I make sure I get them the week before, so I'm not running around at the last minute. If, for whatever reason, they're not in stock, then okay I'll go and get them, but planning is key to maintaining a feeling of ease and flow.

Online grocery shopping isn't perfect. We get substitutes all the time, many of which aren't suitable. Items are not available at all, there are restrictions on how many you can buy of certain product lines and the quality of your food is at the mercy of the picker and packer. Whereas you might go and find an item with a longer shelf life in person, this isn't always considered by the picker. Stuff gets damaged and things get thrown about. Bread gets squashed and milk sometimes leaks. It can become annoying, but I see this as a smaller price to pay than going to the shop myself, especially when we are flat out with work and life in general. You can always select to have no substitutions and return anything that isn't suitable. We get any refunds the next day.

CHRISTMAS GROCERY SHOPPING

From September onwards, I start to order extra bits each week to relieve some of the stress from December. There are lots of things that will store well:

- Cranberry sauce,
- Gravies and sauce mixes,
- Instant stuffing,
- Stock cubes or pots,
- Cornflour,
- Trifle mix,
- Frozen desserts,
- Frozen vegetables,
- Sausages and bacon (I put these together in a tied bag, stick a label on to say they're for Christmas, and put them in the freezer).
- Frozen turkeys are available in some supermarkets from early November. Stick it in the bottom of the freezer and tick it off the list.

Online deliveries for the Christmas period are like playing a game. They get released early, but you need to be quick to get them. I've seen people complaining that they're in a virtual queue to get Christmas delivery slots at the end of November. I've never had an issue with this and it's come down to the fact I have a delivery pass in place, which means I get access to the Christmas delivery slots earlier. I can get these booked well in advance and tend to get one slot booked for each week of December, with a view that I can cancel them if not needed, which frees up a last-minute slot for someone else. Last year, I booked Christmas slots as early as late October, so I've made a note to do the same again this year. The times may vary per store, so check with your supermarket of choice.

As long as the orders are over £40, I can secure the slot. I then amend the shopping list a few days before the delivery, but I write this in my diary, so I don't forget!

BULK BUYING

As well as the general weekly shop, I buy in bulk every four weeks, visiting B&M and Aldi, where I know I can't get items delivered. Some examples of what buy in bulk are:

- Teabags,
- Coffee,
- Vimto (B&M and Iceland Warehouse do 3-litre bottles),
- Chocolate biscuit bars and cakes for packed lunches,
- Crisps,
- Tinned dog food (one of ours has a sensitive tummy so needs Chappie),
- Toilet rolls and kitchen rolls,

- Shampoo, conditioner, shower gels,
- Packet mixes like cornflour and dumpling mixes,
- Stock pots and cubes,
- Bottled sauces and mayonnaise.

And lots of similar items. I buy them in bulk to free up more headspace when I'm ordering the weekly shop. The only downside is where to store it all. We have a large, pine wardrobe in our garage we've named the Armageddon Cupboard. Our overflow stuff goes in here and I can easily keep track of when we start to run low.

Buying in bulk is the best value way to shop. If you haven't got the funds available to fill up an entire cupboard straight away, start small. Try and buy one larger pack of something and knock something else on the head. The week after, something else in a larger pack. Keep going, and the cumulative effect will start to see pounds back in your pocket. It'll take a while but once you get into buying larger quantities, it'll become a habit.

FOOD SUBSCRIPTION BOXES

These are advertised on TV and online as the perfect solution to eating healthier if you have a busy lifestyle.

I've tried some of these and I love the concept, but I've also found them not quite hitting the mark when it comes to catering for larger families. The choice in size range seems to be for two adults, two adults and one child, or two adults and two children. The occasional one will say "feeds five" and I think this is generally two adults and three children of a younger age. I've yet to find one that's marketed as "feeds six, including three hungry teenagers!"

The boxes are great for the fact that it takes the thinking out of the equation. You eat what is sent, everything is weighed out in advance and you just follow the recipe included in the box. Add ingredients, no weighing out. Sorted.

There are issues, however, and excessive packaging is one of them. The number of plastic packets can mount up, and from a cost point of view, we worked out that, price per head, they were more than double what it would cost for us to just buy the food independently. You are paying a premium for the convenience. If having a lower food budget is essential, these aren't the answer.

There's also the doorstep drop-off issue, and how safe that is if you're out of the house. The ones we ordered had ice packs to keep the raw meats cold, but I guess if left for any length of time, that would be an issue, as would whether it would still be there when you get home, depending on your neighbourhood. They are a great concept, but not the answer for everyone.

MAKING LIFE EASY

Have some emergency meals to keep in the freezer or cupboards. They're not to rely on constantly, but more as a back-up for those days when everything has gone wrong and you simply haven't got the capacity to prep anything. You just need something quick to throw in the oven, or open and serve.

The same goes for getting a takeaway if you haven't got the capacity to even boil an egg. The sky won't fall in. Keep some cash to one side for when/if this happens. When we return from a holiday, this is usually what we do as we're exhausted.

YOUR PERSONAL MENU PLANNER

What has been the game changer for me for mealtimes was putting together a menu plan that is well structured, but also flexible. If you count how many minutes you spend with your head in the fridge each night, pondering what to make for tea, it soon adds up. It's not just the time, it's another thing to think about every day. Now is the time to get that under control.

Write down your go-to meals. What do you like eating? What do you like cooking? What can you cook? You don't have to be living off leftovers - this appears to be a bit of a myth about meal plans - nor do you have to eat the same stuff all the time. A meal plan is simply about getting ahead of what you're going to be making for the week or month. It's nothing more complicated than that.

If you're someone who feels they might not fancy what they've got planned, then keep things flexible and you can change it up at any time. Use it as a guide that's going to make shopping, prepping and cooking so much easier.

Consider things like what day of the week it is, how busy you'll be, whether you'll be more tired on a particular day, or whether you've got more time on certain days. You know how long the meals are to make and what you need to do for prep, so consider those when allocating a meal to a particular day.

As an example, a couple of us go to Amateur Dramatics on a Friday evening, so we want something quick and simple to cook. Our Friday evening meal will either be Naan Bread Pizza, Chicken Fajitas or Jacket Potatoes. They're all quick and/or easy to make. We don't tend to have these meals on any other night of the week but if we do, it's the jacket potato for an easy meal when we just haven't got the capacity to cook anything else. It's one hour in the oven and they're sorted. Add a few sides of cheese, beans, tuna, leftover bolognese, or chilli, and everyone is happy.

There are lots of ways you can make mealtimes easier, but having some form or menu plan is the start of it. If it's not something you're used to doing, start slowly. Plan out a few days, or a week if you can manage it. As you become more used to it, try a fortnight. If you can, work up to doing a four-weekly plan.

You might think that sounds boring but remember, we are looking to free up headspace, to take the indecision out of the equation. It's just what we would normally eat anyway, but I've put some thought into balancing meals out throughout the week and making sure we're not on similar meals two days running.

The exception to this is that the kids have pasta on Wednesdays and Thursdays, but that's mainly because we deliberately cook extra pasta and they reheat their own on Thursdays. We'll have fish and rice which they don't want to eat, so it's a quick easy meal for us that's cooked in less than fifteen minutes. It also means the kids are becoming more independent in getting their own meals a couple of times a week.

We also have fish and rice on Tuesdays, so the older ones make something with chips that they can just put in the oven. It's either fish fingers, breaded fish pieces, chicken nuggets, or dippers. I limit this to once a week, perhaps twice if there's no pasta left for Thursdays. It gives us some breathing space and we can see the difference it makes in the kids learning to cook.

They also help with cooking a lot of the other meals. I love the fact that they embrace this and take an interest in the recipes we use. They're learning to check use-by dates, to peel and chop veg efficiently, to cut meat according to how it's going to be cooked and learning about cooking times, food safety and using the hob and oven in a safe way too. They appreciate meal-times a lot more now and are learning invaluable life skills in the process.

ANNUAL MEAL PLAN

For the year, Nic? Really?

Before you start pulling faces, hear me out. If you think about what an annual meal plan is, it's just what you're already doing with a weekly or fortnightly plan but you're multiplying it. I've created ours to consider the changes in season. During winter months, we've got food like casseroles and stews on various nights, amongst the meals we keep constant throughout the year like pasta and fish dishes. We have roast chicken or lamb dinners on a weekend and lots of dishes with mashed potato and carrot with swede.

During the summer months, these change to chicken salads, more rice dishes, using new potatoes instead of mash, chicken and veg traybakes, more use of squashes, and lighter meals in general. We also consider that we'll have a few barbecue meals over the summer.

Check the PDF download collection available via the QR code at the back of the book for a template to help you write your weekly, four-weekly and annual meal plans. It's not as difficult as it sounds.

GOOGLE CALENDAR TIP

I've added all the meals to my Google calendar as an all-day event, so they show up above the date and not at a specific time. This is easy to populate by doing the following:

- For any meals you have the same night every week, create the event and select duplication for once weekly with no end date,
- For any meals you have every two weeks, do the same but select the custom frequency and click fortnightly,
- The same for any meals you have every four weeks, and so on, etc.,
- Once these are all in, manually change any dates you know will be different. For example, birthdays and anniversaries when you might be out or having a specific meal. Change any dates for holidays and meals out. Select to just change that one event though, not the sequence.

So, a quick calendar check means you can see what's for dinner tonight. I've also invited Adrian to the event, so it goes onto his Google calendar. This means he can also check what we're having during the day. Other contractors he's worked with have been slightly bemused on-site when he's checked his phone to see what we're having!

I put this together a while back, not knowing if it was going to be that useful, but I do use it every day. I check it throughout the week and make swaps if needed. Remember, I never set things in stone. It's been a surprisingly helpful exercise to put together.

To round off this chapter, the tasks you can look at undertaking are:

1. If you're not already using online grocery shopping, set up an account and create a basic weekly shopping list. Try one or two deliveries and see how you get on.
2. Create a list of Christmas (or holiday season) shopping items to start buying each week from September or before. Keep all of these in a box or separate cupboard, and check things off once you've bought them.
3. Consider bulk buying. Spend some time shopping in your local area at different shops offering different things. Make the most of buying larger quantities and find somewhere suitable to store them in a garage or separate cupboard.
4. Investigate food subscription boxes to see if they are suitable for you. Most of them offer a large discount for initial orders.

5. Create a weekly menu plan. Increase it to fortnightly, then four-weekly. If you find this is working for you, consider creating an annual one.

What Now?

So we're at the end of the book. As I said right back at the beginning, the chapters I've included don't make up a comprehensive list, there is **so** much more. If I'm being honest, it's top-layer work and if you want to dig deeper and work with me then please get in touch.

But it's a great starting point and hopefully, some inspiration to integrate some systems and structures into your days to help create the business and life you want, whilst keeping your home comfortable and safe.

If I could sum up exactly what you need in three points, it's these:

- Boundaries are vital, with others and yourself,
- Doing the thinking in advance saves time and sanity,
- Everything else can wait whilst you take care of you.

In a nutshell, that's it. The other stuff is just part of the practical things to make these a reality.

However useful you've found this book, I would love to thank you for choosing to pick it up and allow me some time in your day to guide you to a better-organised life. I don't have all the answers and I'm still on my own learning journey, but we're always improving, right?

There's much more work we can do and this is your invitation to come and become part of my world - whether that's hanging out on Facebook or Insta, or working with me directly on either a one-to-one basis or as part of a group membership.

You can join my mailing list by signing up via the QR code at the back of the book.

And via the website which has links to everything:

www.platespinningacademy.co.uk

Keep those plates spinning, but only the bone china ones. The paper and plastic plates will do just fine if they fall. Just pick them back up when you're ready to, if at all.

Much love,

Nic x

facebook.com/nicdaviesuk

instagram.com/platespinningacademy

linkedin.com/in/nic-davies-b4b727233

About the Author

Nic Davies is a productivity and lifestyle mentor, professional speaker and the founder of Platespinning Academy. She helps business owners get life organised at home so they can reclaim the headspace, time and energy needed to grow and run a successful business.

Nic has navigated through adverse times. with hard-hitting curveballs that have forced her to re-assess the importance of self-care and boundaries, as well as becoming more organised in the day-to-day running of her home, business and life in general.

Her mission is to make sure that everyone has an equal opportunity to create a business they love, without feeling held back by household obligations or adversity. She has drawn upon her life experience to build an online community that supports anyone who is struggling to balance home life and business, and empowers them to take control of their time and energy to show up as their best self in all areas of their life.

Fuelled by a passion to see others succeed regardless of obstacles in their way, Nic works with clients on a one-to-one basis, and through free and paid online communities and memberships.

Nic is happiest knee deep in junk at the local car boot sale, or making and creating beautiful things for home and for sale. She always has knitting, jewellery making, painting and all manner of creative projects on the go. Living near Preston in Lancashire, Nic is making the most of semi-rural life whilst working towards a move to the coast.

Workbook

I've created a printable PDF workbook to help you with some of the tasks listed at the end of each chapter. You can do the work without this, but it's a helpful prompt to remind you of the steps you can take that I've identified. Use the QR code below to get it via email.

Printed in Great Britain
by Amazon